A GUIDE TO THE

BUILDINGS
of
BIRMINGHAM

PETER LEATHER

A GUIDE TO THE

BUILDINGS
of
BIRMINGHAM

AN ILLUSTRATED
ARCHITECTURAL HISTORY

TEMPUS

First published 2002

Tempus Publishing Limited
The Mill, Brimscombe Port,
Stroud, Gloucestershire, GL5 2QG

British Library Cataloguing in Publication Data.
A catalogue record for this book is available from the British Library.

ISBN 0 7524 2475 0

Typesetting and origination by Tempus Publishing Limited
Printed in Great Britain by Midway Colour Print, Wiltshire

CONTENTS

FOREWORD AND ACKNOWLEDGEMENTS

This book started life in 1994 as the teaching notes for 'Building History', an adult education class of the University of Birmingham, where I am the Lecturer in Birmingham Studies. Over the years, the notes have been refined, corrected and added to with the help of the many marvellous students who have attended the course and undertaken their own studies of Birmingham buildings – thanks to them all.

In 1998 a second course, entitled 'Birmingham Art & Architecture', was developed as part of a Certificate of Higher Education in Birmingham Studies (the first stage of a degree). For the purposes of the course, and later this book, I was obliged to abandon my original end date of 1900 and come kicking and screaming into the twentieth century (thanks, Nicola!).

My own study of Birmingham buildings could be said to have started in earnest in 1988, four years after I arrived in the city, when I began writing a weekly column on local history for the *Birmingham Daily News*, which became *Birmingham Metronews* in 1991 and the *Birmingham News* in 2002. Buildings have figured large in this, initially as places to visit, but for the past ten years as important and often, sadly, threatened parts of our heritage.

My researches and investigations over the years have brought me into contact with many other people concerned with Birmingham's historic buildings and my knowledge has improved immeasurably as a result. I would especially like to thank the members of Birmingham City Council's Department of Planning Conservation Group; in particular its leader, Chris Hargreaves and his colleagues, Nicola Coxon and Toni Demidowicz. Thanks too to Elizabeth Perkins of the Birmingham Conservation Trust and Rita McLean and her colleagues at Birmingham City Council's Community Museums. I have also learned much over the years from Dianne Barre (who commissioned 'Building History' in the first place), Peter Bennett, George Demidowicz, Andy Foster (currently undertaking the mammoth task of rewriting and vastly extending Pevsner's section on Birmingham city centre), Roy Hartnell, Joe Holyoak, Alex Jones, Roger Lea, Simon Penn, and members of the local Victorian Society and I would like to acknowledge the staff of the Archives and Local Studies & History departments of Birmingham Central Library who have been of enormous help to my students and myself.

A special thank you goes to Mike Hodder, the city planning archaeologist, who read through drafts of the buildings chapters, commenting extensively on the earlier ones and circulating the others to his colleagues in the Conservation Group. As authors must always say at this point, any errors or omissions are entirely down to me!

Finally I would like to thank David Buxton of Tempus for his incredible patience in waiting for my long-overdue manuscript – my students will appreciate the irony of me having to ask for an extension!

HISTORICAL BACKGROUND

The nineteenth- and twentieth-century growth of Birmingham has seen it absorb many neighbouring parishes and manors which all form part of the present-day city. Its architectural heritage, therefore, not only represents 'city' buildings but also 'town', 'village' and 'country' buildings of preceding eras.

Birmingham stands near the national watershed dividing rivers that flow north into the North Sea from those flowing south into the Bristol Channel and can claim to be one of the most land-locked major cities in the world. Its own rivers – the Rea, Tame and Cole – are mere streams and offer no potential for navigation. The principal rivers of the Midlands – Severn, Trent and Avon – form a triangle around the plateau on which Birmingham stands, making it in early times a sort of no-man's land between peoples based in the river valleys. The main geological feature defining the area is a sandstone ridge running southwest to northeast across the city. The point at which this ridge meets an east-west crossing point of the River Rea provides the setting for the origins of Birmingham. It also gives the present-day city centre its well-known elevated position.

To the west of the ridge are Bunter Pebble beds supporting heathland – areas of limited agricultural potential but of great value to Birmingham in the mediaeval period, when they provided grazing land for the cattle trade. To the east of the ridge is Mercian mudstone, thick clay land good for farming, if hard to work, and difficult to cross in wet weather when the clay turned to mud.

Aerial View of Birmingham from the south-west, with the Lickey Hills (part of the national watershed) in the foreground and the sandstone ridge running towards the city centre in the (misty!) distance – the large factory immediately beyond the hills is Longbridge car works.

The city centre from the east, showing its elevated position on the sandstone ridge overlooking the Rea valley.

There has been a human presence in the Birmingham area since the Lower Palaeolithic period, tens or even hundreds of thousands of years ago. Traces of Mesolithic (10,000-4,000 BC) hunter-gatherers have been found in the Tame valley and at least one Neolithic (4,000-2,500 BC) burial mound is known in the city. The Bronze Age (2,500-700 BC) seems to represent a mini boom in population as Birmingham, like other marginal areas such as the Yorkshire Moors and the Highlands of Scotland, benefited from the climate-driven expansion of settlement of the time.

The earlier pattern of human settlement based principally in the Severn, Trent and Avon river valleys with Birmingham as marginal land between was restored in the Iron Age (700 BC - AD 43), at the end of which, with the coming of the Romans, historical light is first cast on the political geography of the region. As might be expected, the three Iron Age territories converted into Roman city-states had their centres well outside the Birmingham area (in Cirencester, Wroxeter near Shrewsbury and Leicester) and only touched it at their very edges.

However, the borderland between three Iron Age territories was the ideal location for an important Roman fort, and this was established at Metchley (now in the grounds of the University of Birmingham and Queen Elizabeth Medical Centre) in around AD 47.

A network of Roman Roads linked Metchley to neighbouring forts at Droitwich, Wall and Alcester – and probably others too. None of these roads seem to have passed through the present city centre, where there was still no significant settlement at this period.

A place actually called Birmingham comes into existence in the Anglo-Saxon period, around AD 600. It has been argued, on highly theoretical grounds, including the status of the place-name, that it may have originated as the home settlement of a family/tribal territory of similar geographical size, but not with the same constituent parts, as the present city.

Whatever the case, Birmingham certainly enters into recorded history, in 1086, in Domesday Book, as a tiny, insignificant manor of little agricultural

Long before there was any such place as Birmingham, Metchley Roman Fort provided the focus for a network of Roman roads, one of which survives in a remarkable state of preservation in Sutton Park and is among the best examples in the country. (Photo by Roy Cleaver)

potential and with a rental value one fifth of immediate neighbours such as Aston and Northfield and one fiftieth of a decent-sized manor in the Avon valley.

The process whereby Birmingham grew from these humble origins to become the third largest town in Warwickshire by the fourteenth century has been much debated by historians. Current thinking has turned away from the conventional view of gradual, organic growth to a more dynamic interpretation, supported to some extent by recent archaeological finds, focusing on the founding of a market, by royal charter, at the Bull Ring in 1166.

It used to be thought that the Bull Ring was the site of the original Anglo-Saxon village of Birmingham, chosen because of its well-drained, elevated location and its proximity to an important crossing-point of the River Rea. Instead, it may have remained unoccupied until the twelfth century when a new market town was created to attract trade – despite the inadequacies of the river crossing – to a manor whose only hope of success lay in commercial growth.

The new town was furnished with a moated manor house (now buried beneath the wholesale markets) and a Norman church, fragments of which were discovered during demolition in advance of building the present church in the 1870s. The town's only religious house, the Priory/Hospital of St Thomas is first recorded in the thirteenth century, although it may have existed earlier.

The market foundation was clearly a huge success – tax returns of 1327 show Birmingham almost the equal of Warwick and only lagging behind Coventry, then one of the top five towns in the country.

Growth was, if anything, enhanced rather than hampered by the Black Death, when weaker local markets fell by the wayside, reducing the competition. It continued throughout the fifteenth century, although the physical development of the town was constrained by a surrounding belt of manorial and priory lands.

These twin impediments to expansion were removed in the 1530s when the feudal de Bermingham family came to an end, to be replaced by more commercially minded owners, and the priory lands became available for investment following the dissolution of the monasteries by Henry VIII.

Opposite: Excavations in advance of the redevelopment of the Bull Ring have shown that the city centre originated as a planned new market town in the twelfth century.

Families who had made their money as merchants or graziers in the profitable Welsh cattle trade were now able to buy the freed-up manorial and priory lands, and establish private estates. The best known of these is the Colmore Estate, to the northwest of the centre, which later became Birmingham's Jewellery Quarter.

Commercial activities were still the main source of new money in Birmingham in the early seventeenth century when Thomas Holte, whose fortune was based on trade, built the magnificent Aston Hall. But a new source of wealth was on the horizon with the spread down the Tame Valley of blast furnaces and forges for large-scale iron production. The Jennens, whose fine mid-seventeenth-century townhouse on High Street sadly no longer exists, could be said to be the first Birmingham family to make their fortune from industry.

A split between the land-owning and manufacturing/mercantile classes in Birmingham society became apparent during the Civil War. The town itself was staunchly Parliamentarian; but Royalist Thomas Holte was

The mediaeval priory of St Thomas has left no trace but is depicted on this 1960s plaque in Old Square – its lands, freed up by the Reformation, provided vital building land when the town expanded in the eighteenth century.

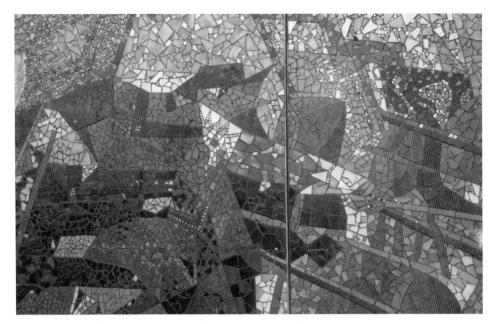

The English Civil War, commemorated by this mosaic of the 1643 'Battle of Birmingham' (recently buried during redevelopment of Colmore Circus), had two major effects on the town: the destruction caused by Prince Rupert hastened the replacement of timber-framed by brick buildings; while, on a more positive note, the market for swords and pikes, and later guns, provided by the war seems to have kick-started local industry and prompted an economic and population boom in the second half of the century.

proud to accommodate Charles I at Aston Hall on his march down to Edge Hill in October 1642.

Prince Rupert's attack on Birmingham in April 1643, partly directed at disrupting the making of swords and pikes for Parliament, caused the destruction of about one tenth of the town. In architectural terms, it hastened the replacement of timber-framed by brick buildings.

Despite the ravages of war, Birmingham flourished in the aftermath, experiencing exceptional population growth in the late seventeenth century. This has traditionally been ascribed to the arrival of large numbers of Nonconformists in the town, escaping persecution elsewhere; but it is now felt that the size of this influx has been overestimated and that the cause must be sought elsewhere. One possibility is that the conversion of Birmingham's sword and pike makers to the new technology of guns drew many skilled craftsmen to the town.

Whatever the reason, by the end of the century Birmingham had finally overtaken its old rival, Coventry, and established itself beyond dispute as the master of the Midlands.

The growth in industry and population gathered pace in the eighteenth century with the Digbeth/Deritend area in particular becoming a centre of manufacture. Old 'agricultural' industries such as smithing, nailmaking and leatherworking gradually moved out into the surrounding countryside to be replaced by new 'manufacturing' industries such as gunmaking and metalworking.

Growth in both the size and the prosperity of the population and the consequent demand for more and better housing finally forced the town to expand beyond its mediaeval boundaries. Early eighteenth century development centred on the so-called 'High Town', uphill from the Bull Ring, with Birmingham's first Georgian square, called simply 'The Square' (later Old Square) and the first new church to be created out of the mediaeval parish of St Martin – St Philip's.

The former priory and manorial lands bought up by the town's wealthiest families in the sixteenth century now became prime development sites. Typical of this was the Colmore Estate, developed into a high-class residential area from 1746 onwards.

The same thing happened to the Weaman Estate to its north and the Jennens Estate on the opposite (east) side of town. Each was provided with a new church.

Towards the end of the century, and especially during the Napoleonic wars, the building boom temporarily subsided, with houses on the new Bradford Estate proving hard to shift and the town's most prestigious building project, The Crescent off Broad Street, remaining unfinished.

Eighteenth-century Birmingham was a mostly peaceable place with different elements of society getting along together – something that was to prove immensely important when the town began to assert itself politically in the nineteenth century – but the century ended with one of the worst periods of rioting in the city's history. The so-called Priestley Riots of 1791 against scientist/theologian Joseph Priestley and others who shared his liberal views on the French Revolution, saw the destruction of Nonconformist Meeting Houses and the homes of the victims.

Already by this time, industry was creeping out of Digbeth/Deritend and invading the new residential areas. Gunmakers had begun to move into the

Weaman Estate as early as mid-century, converting houses and infilling back gardens with workshops. By the end of the century jewellers had begun to do the same to the Colmore Estate.

The jewellery trade had in part grown out of the town's most important 'new' industry: brass. The application of Birmingham's long-established metalworking skills to brass is considered by many historians to have been the making of the place.

The mass production of small brass items, then known as 'toys' e.g. buckles, buttons, boxes and trinkets was ideally suited to the new 'conveyor belt' working practices of the time.

However, Birmingham did not at this stage develop large factories based on new technology of the type found in Manchester and the rest of the north, but rather expanded the already existing system of interconnected workshops using stamp, press, lathe and draw-bench.

Typical of this was the town's most famous 'Industrial Revolution' period site, the Soho Manufactory – not a production-line factory in the northern sense but

The Industrial Revolution starts here! Nothing remains aboveground of Matthew Boulton's epoch-making Soho Manufactory but his Soho Foundry of 1796 (where James Watt's steam engines were built) remains relatively intact in neighbouring Smethwick and is hoped to be developed as a heritage site.

a bringing together of skilled craftsmen using simple hand technology under the one roof. It is perhaps the greatest irony of Birmingham's history that the Boulton-Watt steam engines so famously developed at Soho were initially of little use in the town itself, being more suited to powering large machinery.

The enormous growth in the mass production of small items ideally suited to export meant that the town had to do something about its communications with the outside world. As one of the most landlocked places in England, with no navigable rivers, Birmingham had been forced to rely on a network of mediaeval road links. Despite improvements through turnpiking, the roads could not cope with the huge quantity of raw materials coming into the town and finished goods going out.

For this reason, Matthew Boulton, the founder of Soho, and other local manufacturers were eager to embrace the new phase of canal building intro-

The canals converging at Gas Street Basin made land-locked Birmingham the very centre of the national waterways network in the late eighteenth and early nineteenth centuries, and represent one of the city's greatest achievements.

duced by James Brindley. The Birmingham Canal of 1767-72 was one of the first in the country and proved such a success – for example halving the price of Black Country coal – that it spawned many more. By the end of the century, the most land-locked town in England had transformed itself into the very epicentre of the national waterways network.

The 'trick' was repeated in the mid-nineteenth century when Birmingham became the heart of the nation's railways, and again in the twentieth with the motorways.

As a result of all the remarkable achievements of the eighteenth century, Birmingham entered the nineteenth as a major industrial and population centre with over 70,000 inhabitants. However, it still had no proper local government and no parliamentary representation (although between 1774 and 1796 one of the Warwickshire county MPs was always, by agreement, a 'Birmingham' man).

The problem of uncontrolled building and a growing need for public facilities had led in 1769 to the formation of a Street Commission, initially responsible for fairly mundane tasks such as keeping the streets swept and lit and looking after the markets. But as time went on it became more ambitious and provided Birmingham with its first real public buildings: the Public Offices in Moor Street, the Town Hall and the Market Hall.

This though did not solve the need for the town to be properly governed and represented. The cause was taken up by local banker, Thomas Attwood, who took advantage of the greater social cohesion than in other industrial towns (due to less divisive working practices) to form a 'union of classes': the Birmingham Political Union. A series of mass meetings in the town helped push through the Reform Act of 1832, whereby Birmingham was given its first two MPs (one of them Attwood).

In his role as MP, Attwood played a part in the passage of the 1835 Municipal Corporations Act, as a result of which Birmingham was able to apply for the status of a borough with elected council, granted in 1838.

The early years of the council were hampered (until 1842) by legal wrangling over the legitimacy of the Charter by local Tories (who had not won a single seat in the first elections) and (until 1851) by the continued existence of the Street Commission. Things got no better when these were resolved due to a split in the Liberal governing party between 'extravagants' – who wanted to raise rates in order to provide Birmingham with the

Winson Green prison and the adjoining asylum and workhouse form a sorry trio of institutions reminding us of the Dickensian 'hard times' of Birmingham's early Victorian history before Joseph Chamberlain made it 'the Best Governed City in the World' in the 1870s.

sort of public facilities then being built elsewhere in the country – and 'economists' – who wanted above all to keep the rates down. The latter were in the ascendancy for much of the 1850s and '60s, causing Birmingham to fall farther and farther behind other large towns. At a time when museums, art galleries, public baths and parks were being established elsewhere in the country, all Birmingham had to show by way of public works were the Borough Gaol and Asylum which, together with the Board of Guardians' Workhouse, formed a sorry trio of institutions at the very edge of the town in Winson Green.

National initiatives towards sanitation, improved medical services and the taking into public ownership of water and gas were all ignored.

Things began to change in the 1860s under the pressure of public opinion generated by local Nonconformist ministers preaching the 'Civic Gospel' – the idea that towns like churches should use money collected from richer members of the community to provide a better life for all. The first 'victory' for this new philosophy was the belated adoption of the 1850 Free Libraries

Act but it only came to full fruition with the landslide victory of Joseph Chamberlain in the mayoral elections of 1873.

Chamberlain had first become involved in local politics through his membership of the Birmingham Education Society, which played a leading role in the campaign for universal primary education leading to the Act of 1870. Unsurprisingly, Birmingham was at the forefront of constructing the new 'Board' schools required by the act and is generally regarded as having the best in the country.

In three remarkable years, Chamberlain transformed the town, not only catching up with the rest of the country but also taking the lead in many areas. The work he started led to Birmingham being dubbed 'The Best Governed City in the World' by an American magazine in 1890.

The long delayed 'municipalisations' (taking into municipal ownership) of gas and water were a huge success, the former generating money for projects such as a new Art Gallery and Museum. The policy was later extended to electricity and public transport, and the town also established the country's first municipal institute of higher education, the College (later School) of Art.

A new road, Corporation Street, was cut through the heart of the town and lined with shops and hotels. At the top end it eventually housed Birmingham's new Law Courts, one of several signs of growing status in the 1880s and '90s along with becoming a City in 1889 and having a Lord Mayor from 1896.

Chamberlain's influence on Birmingham continued long after his move into national government in 1876. He was instrumental in the establishment of the University of Birmingham in 1900, refusing to countenance a federation of provincial universities and insisting that Birmingham should be based on the more academically independent Scottish model.

His long-term goal to provide the city with a constant water supply was finally realised in 1904 with the opening of the seventy-three-mile-long Elan Valley Aqueduct from Wales.

On a spiritual level, the creation of its own bishopric and the elevation of St Philip's to a cathedral in 1905 further enhanced Birmingham's status.

In the same year, carmaker Herbert Austin opened his factory at Longbridge; but he was not Birmingham's first motor pioneer. Ten years earlier, Frederick William Lanchester had built Britain's first four-wheeled, petrol-driven motorcar in the city.

The Longbridge works marked the culmination of a trend whereby Birmingham had finally moved away from small workshops in the crowded streets of the city centre towards large factories in the 'greenbelt' beyond. The most famous instance was, of course, the establishment of the Cadbury factory at Bournville in 1879.

Cadburys were not the first local employers to build workers' housing around their isolated premises, but they took the concept to a new level. They created a whole village of high quality housing and a healthy amount of open space, thereby inspiring to a great extent the garden city movement of the early twentieth century.

As a result of the expansion of Birmingham industry and housing into surrounding areas, a movement arose for the creation of a Greater Birmingham incorporating all these new 'suburbs' in the city. Although initially opposed by the neighbouring county councils, conscious of the rateable value of these districts, the Greater Birmingham Act was passed in 1911, vastly expanding the city's extent and population and making it beyond doubt the nation and the Empire's Second City.

The expansion of council services and the new opportunities thereby offered finally tempted Joseph Chamberlain's son, Neville, initially reluctant, into local politics. Lord Mayor in 1915-16 before following his late father's footsteps into national government, he initiated a public ownership scheme arguably more revolutionary than anything Joe had ever done: the Birmingham Municipal Bank.

The inter-war years saw Birmingham filling up its new suburbs with vast housing estates – that at Kingstanding was bigger than Shrewsbury! As Chancellor of the Exchequer in 1933, Neville Chamberlain opened Birmingham's 40,000th council house on the Bournville-inspired Weoley Castle estate. Perhaps this goes some way to explain his unfairly condemned reluctance to enter into a war that would do so much damage to his beloved city.

Between August 1940 and April 1943 Birmingham was hit by more high explosives than any British city, other than London and Liverpool/Birkenhead. Over 2,000 people died in sixty-five air raids. A number of important buildings, including the Market Hall and St Thomas church, were ruined along with some

Opposite: Chamberlain Square, in honour of Joseph Chamberlain, who was Mayor from 1873 to 1876, and whose many successes included the 'municipalisation' of water (hence the fountain) and gas (which paid for the Museum and Art Gallery behind).

Remembrance: since it was built in the 1920s the 'Colonnades' has been a place to reflect on the victims of war. Originally it faced the Hall of Memory in what is now Centenary Square but was relocated in the 1990s to form part of the St Thomas Peace Garden in Bath Row.

12,000 homes. But that still left a legacy from Victorian times of over 50,000 substandard houses to be dealt with after the war.

Post-war restrictions delayed building work even further, meaning thousands of prefabs had to be erected. Even when funds were available, new legislation to prevent Birmingham expanding farther into the greenbelt forced the council to abandon its garden city principles and put up the hated high-rise flats.

The post-war years were of course the age of the high-rise, with office blocks going up by the dozen in the city centre and beyond, dwarfing earlier buildings. The trend continues to this day. The 'Americanisation' of Birmingham was further enhanced by construction of an Inner Ring Road girdling the city centre with a mixture of underpasses and circuses, the dehumanising effects of which are only now being removed. It is perhaps fitting that the most potent symbol of this phase, the Bull Ring Centre has been demolished at the turn of the new Millennium.

Centenary Square, opened to coincide with the 100th anniversary of Birmingham's grant of city status in 1889, is the new heart of a city where business, tourism and leisure are supplementing and replacing the old manufacturing industries that made it great.

The 1970s and '80s brought economic crisis to Birmingham's age-old manufacturing industries with famous names such as BSA, Chad Valley and Fort Dunlop all folding. Factory buildings of all eras and architectural styles became redundant.

When revival came in the 1990s, under a once more bullish city council dubbed in the *Financial Times* 'the inheritors of Chamberlain', it was a new world of service industries, heritage and tourism typified by the International Convention Centre and adjacent Hyatt Regency hotel.

Centenary Square, named for the 100th anniversary of city status in 1989, is the heart of this new Birmingham. But the old heart, at the Bull Ring, still beats, with massive redevelopment aimed at reviving the place where it all started so long ago.

27

ANCIENT AND MEDIAEVAL
BUILDINGS AND STRUCTURES

THERE ARE NO 'buildings' as such in Birmingham predating the Norman Conquest but earlier structures do survive, while others have been revealed by archaeology. First among these, on present knowledge, is Kingstanding Mound, a much-abused Late Neolithic/Early Bronze Age burial mound from around 2500 BC. Claims of another such mound in Sutton Park have recently been disproved, but eighteenth-century peat digging revealed a possible Neolithic/Bronze Age timber trackway there.

Far more significant are the city's Bronze Age 'Burnt Mounds', around forty of which have so far been identified. Dating from around 1200 BC and believed to be either cooking sites or saunas, their study by local archaeologists has made them internationally known.

Birmingham's first Iron Age site, a farmstead at Langley Mill Farm in Sutton Coldfield, was discovered during excavations in advance of road building in 2001. The site continued to be occupied into the Roman period, when an important fort was established at Metchley (now buried beneath the University of Birmingham and Queen Elizabeth Medical Centre). Excavations in recent years have shown that the fort was occupied by up to 1,000 troops from shortly after the Roman Invasion of AD 43 and continued in various forms until the early third century. A short-lived attempt at reconstruction in the 1950s has left behind only a corner of the earth rampart and the stumps of what was a timber tower.

Metchley was linked to neighbouring Roman forts by a network of roads, one of which survives in a remarkable state of preservation in Sutton Park and is among the best examples in the country.

It may not look much but Kingstanding burial mound is the oldest man-made structure currently known in Birmingham, dating from the late Neolithic or early Bronze Age (around 2500 BC).

Although many people think of it as an entirely modern city, Birmingham has important ancient sites, including some internationally known Bronze Age burnt mounds – this one, at Langley Mill Farm in Sutton Coldfield, was unearthed during road-building operations in 2001 and subsequently destroyed, but many others remain.

The northwest corner of the Roman Fort at Metchley was rebuilt in the 1950s but its timber breastwork and tower (the stumps of which are still visible) have since been removed.

Structural evidence for the Anglo-Saxon period is slight. The most significant site (although just outside the city) is possibly Castle Bromwich, where an Anglo-Saxon palisaded enclosure underlies the Norman motte. Traces of pits and hearths excavated at Weoley Castle are alleged to be pre-Conquest. Despite the claims of various church guidebooks, there is no firm evidence of Anglo-Saxon architecture in any of the city's mediaeval churches. A large stone slab found beneath Harborne Parish Church has been claimed to be the base of an Anglo-Saxon cross – this is doubtful but Harborne has been identified for historical reasons as one of the likeliest sites for an Anglo-Saxon minster in the city.

The oldest extant church architectural remains in Birmingham are at Northfield, which has a re-sited twelfth-century Norman doorway among other features. A similar doorway is known to have existed at Aston (another candidate for an Anglo-Saxon minster). Architectural fragments discovered in Birmingham Parish Church during Victorian rebuilding also date from this period. Norman windows exist at Handsworth and Kings Norton.

There are eleven fully or partially surviving mediaeval parish churches or chapels in Birmingham. To these can be added a fourteenth-century chapel at

Just outside the city boundaries, the Norman castle at Castle Bromwich, whose motte survives alongside the M6 motorway, played an important part in Birmingham's early history.

Despite claims of an Anglo-Saxon origin for several of Birmingham's mediaeval churches and an alleged, but unlikely, Anglo-Saxon cross-base in the grounds of St Peter's, Harborne, the oldest verifiable church architecture in the city is Norman. This fine twelfth-century doorway at St Laurence, Northfield is an example.

The tomb of nineteenth-century Birmingham architect, Thomas Rickman, whose 1817 book *An Attempt to Discriminate the Styles of Architecture in England* established the terms Early English, Decorated and Perpendicular.

The unspoiled thirteenth-century Early English chancel at St Laurence, Northfield is one of the finest in the Midlands, if not the whole country.

Deritend, rebuilt in the eighteenth century and demolished in the 1960s; a sixteenth century chapel at Ward End, thought to have been totally rebuilt in the 1830s and a fifteenth-century timber-framed chapel, encased in brick in the eighteenth century, at Castle Bromwich, which, although in the mediaeval parish of Aston, is no longer within the city bounds.

All the styles of mediaeval church architecture are represented in the city – indeed it was a Birmingham-based architect, Thomas Rickman, whose tomb can be seen in the former churchyard of his St George's, Newtown (demolished 1960), who first established the terms 'Early English', 'Decorated' and 'Perpendicular'.

In addition to its aforementioned Norman features, St Laurence, Northfield can boast an almost unspoilt thirteenth-century Early English chancel. St Nicolas, Kings Norton also has a thirteenth-century chancel (although much altered) but its finest features are the fourteenth-century Decorated nave and aisles and fifteenth-century tower and spire.

St Edburgha's, Yardley may have Anglo-Saxon origins (the name comes from King Alfred's granddaughter, via Pershore Abbey, whose ownership of

The fifteenth-century tower and spire at St Nicolas, Kings Norton may be one of three in the city built by the Henry Ulm named on an inscription of 1461 at St Giles, Sheldon. The timber-framed building to the left of the church is the late fifteenth-century Saracen's Head.

Yardley is confirmed by a charter of 972) but the earliest surviving features are thirteenth century. Its fifteenth-century tower and spire closely resemble that of Kings Norton and both may have been built by Henry Ulm, whose work on the equally similar tower (without a spire) at St Giles, Sheldon is recorded in an inscription of 1461. Sheldon is otherwise almost entirely four-teenth century Decorated, although much restored.

Also heavily restored is Holy Trinity, Sutton Coldfield, whose thirteenth-century origins are only visible in the plinth and remains of shallow buttresses at the east end, while the tower is mid-fifteenth and the 'Vesey' (see later) chancel chapels early sixteenth.

Mediaeval church towers survived Victorian rebuilding at St Mary's Handsworth (twelfth or thirteenth century), St Peter's, Harborne (late four-teenth or fifteenth) and, most magnificently, at St Peter and Paul, Aston (fifteenth century).

Sadly, the least well preserved of the city's surviving mediaeval churches is the parish church of Birmingham itself, St Martin's in the Bull Ring. The base of the tower contains stonework from the thirteenth century, when the present church is thought to have originated, but fragments of reused Norman deco-ration found during rebuilding in the 1870s hint at something earlier.

Later mediaeval church architecture is best represented by St Mary's, Moseley which, although rebuilt in the eighteenth and nineteenth centuries, retains its fifteenth-century Perpendicular style and tower from around 1500. St Bartholomew's, Edgbaston also has a sixteenth-century tower, although both this and the church's earlier mediaeval features were badly damaged in the Civil War and required extensive rebuilding afterwards.

The city's most poignant piece of sixteenth-century church architecture is the Perpendicular 'Rose and Pomegranate' door at St Edburgha's, Yardley, said to commemorate the doomed marriage of Henry VIII (Rose) and Catherine of Aragon (Pomegranate) or possibly Catherine's earlier marriage to Prince Arthur, which caused all the trouble!

Mediaeval Birmingham supported only one monastic house, the Hospital/Priory of St Thomas (first recorded 1286), which was totally demol-ished following dissolution, leaving only a single carved stone in the collec-tion of Birmingham Museum and a commemorative plaque in Old Square.

Opposite: The magnificent fifteenth-century tower and spire at St Peter and Paul, Aston (a church which may have Anglo-Saxon origins) is a landmark for motorists on the nearby M6.

The sixteenth-century 'Rose and Pomegranate' door at St Edburgha's, Yardley is thought to commemorate one of the doomed marriages of Catherine of Aragon to either Henry VIII or his older brother, Arthur.

Other 'priories' (e.g. Colebrook) and 'abbeys' (e.g. Metchley and Hockley) are the results of a nineteenth-century affectation to live in a former monastic site, although local myths of ghostly hooded monks abound!

Birmingham also possesses a surprising number of secular mediaeval structures. The Norman motte and bailey castle at Castle Bromwich is just outside the city but there is a ruined thirteenth-century stone fortified manor house at Weoley Castle (with earlier phases beneath) and a number of 'moated sites', dating from between 1150 and 1500. Built for status rather than defence, the best preserved are Kent's Moat, Sheldon (probably fourteenth century and now, not as incongruously as it might seem, surrounding a group of 1960s flats and maisonettes), Peddimore Hall, Sutton Coldfield (first recorded 1247 but the house is from around 1660) and New Hall, Sutton Coldfield.

This last is a magnificent multi-period house originating in the thirteenth century (grey-white masonry), much expanded in the sixteenth (red sandstone) and further developed in the eighteenth and nineteenth (for example the 'Gothick tower of 1796' and the Victorian parapets).

The moated manor house known as Weoley Castle (from which the 1920s/30s housing estate surrounding it takes its name) was built in stone following the granting of a 'licence to crenellate' in 1264 but had existed since the twelfth century or even earlier.

New Hall, Sutton Coldfield, dating back to the thirteenth century (but with a 'Gothick' eighteenth-century tower and nineteenth-century battlements) is the finest of the many mediaeval moated sites within the city and is now a prestige hotel.

Clearly visible moated sites can also be found in Perry Park (now the boating pool) and Hawkesley Farm (surrounding a 1950s tower block).

Excavations on the site of Birmingham Moat revealed a typologically early structure and architectural fragments, which may tie in with the presumed creation of a new town around the Bull Ring in the later twelfth century.

The most remarkable mediaeval structures in the city are perhaps the 'Vesey' houses of Sutton Coldfield, fifty-one of which (according to the inscription on his tomb in the parish church) were built by Bishop Vesey, a local man who rose to prominence in the church, in the first half of the sixteenth century.

So far twenty-one of these houses have been identified (eight demolished) but others may survive behind later facades. The houses, with their distinctive 'ahead of their time' features of external stone chimneys, fireplaces on every floor, internal spiral staircases, and ashlar quoins and mullioned windows, are variously interpreted as homes for weavers brought to the town by Vesey to boost the local economy, watch-houses on the approach roads or even a rehousing of the entire population.

Vesey Cottage on Wylde Green Road, Sutton Coldfield is a typical example of the remarkable stone houses built by Bishop Vesey, a native of the area, in the first half of the sixteenth century.

The best examples are Old Farm, Moor Hall Drive (traditionally Vesey's birthplace), Vesey Cottage near New Hall Mill on Wylde Green Road, Ye Olde Stone House next to St Peter's church on Maney Hill Road, Warren House Farm off Walmley Road, and High Heath Cottage in the fields off Withy Hill Road.

Vesey is also credited with the surviving stone bridge of around 1520 at Water Orton.

The Vesey houses are so exceptional in Birmingham because its mediaeval domestic architecture was otherwise almost entirely timber-framed, with not even the stone cellars so common in nearby Coventry. The oldest such buildings are claimed – but without scientific dating – to be fourteenth-century cruck-frames at Minworth Greaves (re-erected at Bournville in 1929-32) and The Lad in the Lane, Erdington (said to have the date 1306 carved on one of its timbers). Selly Manor (also re-erected at Bournville) is a box-frame building, which may in part date back to the same century (based on stylistic dating of walls in open framing). Thirteenth-century roof-tiles have been found in archaeological excavations around the Bull Ring.

Cruck-framed Minworth Greaves (in the background) and box-framed Selly Manor, re-erected at Bournville by the Cadburys in the early twentieth century, are both claimed on stylistic grounds to originate in the fourteenth century, but they have never been scientifically dated.

New Shipton Barn (1425) and this building, the Old Smithy (1442-44), both in Sutton Coldfield, are, thanks to dendrochronology (tree-ring dating), the oldest securely dated timber-framed buildings in Birmingham.

The Old Grammar School in the churchyard of St Nicolas, Kings Norton, with its late fifteenth-century timber-framed upper storey and sixteenth-century brick ground floor (presumably it wasn't built in that order!) is the city's most appealing mediaeval building.

The Old Crown, Deritend is Birmingham's best-known timber-framed building and the only one remaining in the city centre – its traditional date of 1368 has been disproved by architectural experts who believe it was built around 1500 as the Guild Hall and School of the vanished church of St John.

The earliest securely dated buildings (through dendrochronology/tree-ring dating) are the cruck-framed New Shipton Barn (1425) and Old Smithy (1442-44), both in Sutton Coldfield. Dendro-dates have also been obtained from the barn at the original Minworth Greaves site (1450-75) and re-used timbers in the barn at Monyhull (1466-1501). Fifteenth-century dates are assigned to the cruck-framed Handsworth Old Town Hall and (end of fifteenth century) the close-studded Old Grammar School and Saracen's Head, Kings Norton, and Old Trust School, Yardley. The Old Crown, Deritend, traditionally dated to 1368, is actually from around 1500 and may well have been built as the priest's house, guildhall and school of St John's, Deritend. This role and consequent association with the Protestant martyr John Rogers has usually been assigned to the Golden Lion, which formerly stood on the opposite side of Deritend from the Old Crown and was re-located to Cannon Hill Park in 1911 – but this is stylistically a later sixteenth-century building.

Blakesley Hall, Yardley, tree-ring dated to 1590, is Birmingham's finest timber-framed building and now a museum – it has both architectural and family links to another city building, Stratford House (1601).

Also of this period is the impressive Blakesley Hall, Yardley, dendro-dated to 1590. Stratford House on Camp Hill, which has family connections and architectural similarities to Blakesley, has the date 1601 on its porch. These, together with the subsequently stuccoed Pype Hayes Hall, thought to have been built during the reign of James I (1603-25), are the last high status timber-framed buildings in Birmingham, but the timber framing at Bell's Farm in Kings Norton may be contemporary with the brick chimneys, which bear a date-stone of 1661.

SIXTEENTH- TO EIGHTEENTH-
CENTURY BRICK BUILDINGS

I N 1538 A DYNASTIC marriage took place between the Este family of Hay Hall in Tyseley and the Gibbons family of New Hall in Sutton Coldfield. It is possible that this event provides the context for a major refurbishment of Hay Hall, which saw the fifteenth-century timber-framed building refaced in the fashionable new material, brick. If this is so, it makes Hay Hall, now hidden away in an industrial zone but beautifully restored in the 1980s, the oldest brick building in Birmingham.

More securely dated is Sheldon Hall, where the central section of a sixteenth-century timber-frame was replaced by a brick building whose roof rafters have been dendro-dated to 1616. However, there is strong historical evidence for Castle Bromwich Hall, just outside the city, having been rebuilt in brick in around 1599.

Aston Hall (1618-35) completes the transition from timber to brick, although even here experts would argue that it is essentially a timber-framed building with a brick facing. The fact that this Jacobean country house has survived to the present day relatively unaltered makes it of great architectural importance.

The grandly named Lifford Hall is in fact a brick watermill and house of the first half of the seventeenth century replacing an earlier timber-frame – it was extended to a size more befitting the name, with a large banqueting room and 'Gothick' garden features in the 1860s.

The plans and styles of these early brick buildings are, as elsewhere, still strongly influenced by mediaeval conventions. The first true 'Renaissance'

Hay Hall, Tyseley may have been refaced in brick at the time of a dynastic marriage in 1538, which, if true, would make it Birmingham's oldest brick building.

The central block of Sheldon Hall is the earliest securely dated brick building in Birmingham, based on a tree-ring date for the roof rafters of 1616.

Aston Hall (1618-35) completes the transition from timber-framing to brick in the fashionable Dutch style of the time; its Jacobean architecture has survived relatively intact because the house was unoccupied in Victorian times and was in fact one of the first old houses to be opened as a museum when acquired by private owners in 1858 and then taken over by the corporation in 1864.

(some would say 'Wrenaissance') building in the city is the Moat House, Sutton Coldfield, of 1679, built by Warwickshire architect, Sir William Wilson (best known for rebuilding St Mary's, Warwick after the Great Fire of 1694), who lived there. He had previously lived at Langley Hall (demolished) off Ox Leys Road, where the stable block of around 1685, which forms the present Hall, is almost certainly his work.

Wilson is also credited, with increasing certainty, with building Birmingham's first Classical (Queen Anne) church, the Ascension in Hall Green, in 1704 (the chancel, transepts and upper tower were built in 1860). The rebuilt St Mary and St Margaret, Castle Bromwich (1726-31 by Thomas White) is in a similar style, if more baroque.

Birmingham can boast one of the finest English Baroque churches in the country in the shape of St Philip's (1709-1715, tower 1725) by Thomas Archer – since 1905 it has been better known as Birmingham Cathedral.

The Moat House in Sutton Coldfield (1679) is the first true Renaissance building in Birmingham and was designed by noted Warwickshire architect, Sir William Wilson, as his home.

St Philip's and St Martin's are two of the three landmark buildings visible on the Westley Prospects of 1732, the first contemporary and relatively true to life visual depiction of the town. The third, the Georgian rebuilding of the sixteenth-century King Edward VI Grammar School, was itself replaced in Victorian times, but some idea of its appearance can be gained from the surviving eighteenth-century parts of its contemporary in Sutton Coldfield, the Bishop Vesey Grammar School (1729).

A high-class residential district, the 'High Town' developed around St Philip's, the last remnants of which were swept away in the 1950s. There was also a fine Georgian square to the north (known originally simply as 'The Square' and later 'Old Square'), designed by the aforementioned William Westley in 1713. The last vestige of this is a panelled room from one of the houses re-erected at Aston Hall.

The Church of the Ascension, Hall Green started life as Job Marston's Chapel in 1704 and was almost certainly also built by Sir William Wilson – the chancel, transepts and upper tower were added in 1860.

St Philip's Church (since 1905 Birmingham Cathedral) was built by nationally important English Baroque architect Thomas Archer in 1709-1715 (tower added 1725).

The Johnson Room at Aston Hall is a re-erected room from one of the houses on The Square, an early eighteenth-century development in the town centre; it is so named because Dr Samuel Johnson was a frequent visitor to the house.

The eighteenth century saw a considerable expansion of building in and around central Birmingham with a series of Georgian residential suburbs developing around the mediaeval core. Unfortunately, this Georgian 'growth-ring' around the edge of the sandstone ridge on which the city centre stands, was in the path of the Inner Ring Road built in the 1960s and much was destroyed.

The one survivor is St Paul's Square (constructed between 1780-90), at the heart of the Colmore Estate, with its church by Roger Eykyns (1777-79, with the belfry and spire added in 1822-23), based on St Martin-in-the-Fields in London. The painted (not stained) glass East Window by Francis Eginton is especially noteworthy.

There were once similar Georgian estate churches at St Mary's (1774) on the Weaman Estate and St Bartholomew's (1749) on the Jennens Estate but they have long since been demolished. Some of the 1750s buildings on Bartholomew Row, which faced the church, survive today, although they were greatly altered in the nineteenth century, as Christopher Wray's Lighting

St Paul's Square (built around 1780-90) is the sole survivor of a series of Georgian housing estates that developed around the town centre in the eighteenth century but were swept away by the building of the Inner Ring Road in the 1960s.

Company. The Bull pub on Loveday Street in the Gun Quarter, just round the corner from where St Mary's used to stand, has a tripartite Venetian window and other architectural elements betraying its origins as a group of late eighteenth-century houses.

Speculative Georgian development continued until brought to an end by the Napoleonic Wars but little survives bar a few houses on the Bradford Street estate (1771). Nothing at all remains of Birmingham's grandest Georgian building scheme, 'The Crescent'. Started in 1788 as a prestige residential development of twenty-three houses and a central chapel, building halted in 1795 with less than half of them completed. The scheme was not continued after the wars because by then, contrary to the 'estate agent's blurb' that 'There is not the least possibility of any future buildings ever excluding the inhabitants from a most agreeable prospect of the country', the area, adjacent to the new canals, was awash with industry. The completed part of 'The Crescent' survived until the 1980s and bequeathed its name to a local theatre that started life there.

49

Georgian 'country' houses in what are now inner-city suburbs have fared little better, the one great exception being 'Farm' in Sparkbrook, the home of the Lloyd banking family, built probably in the 1740s. Some houses of this period do survive farther out, notably: Edgbaston Hall (1717), on the site of earlier halls; Rookery House, Erdington (around 1725-30), replacing and to some extent mimicking an earlier timber-framed hall-house; Monyhull and Witton Halls (1730s); the Royal Hotel (around 1750) and various other buildings on High Street and Coleshill Street, Sutton Coldfield; and Maryvale, Oscott (around 1753). All that survives of the early eighteenth-century Moseley Hall (preceding the Greek Revival building mentioned in Chapter 5) is its dovecote and 'cowhouse'. However, the nearby Moseley Park, formed out of the Hall's grounds, contains an intact 1790s ice house, and there are the remains of another, dating from around 1776 beside the River Tame, off Garden Grove, Hamstead in what were once the grounds of the vanished Hamstead Hall.

More modest dwellings of the seventeenth and eighteenth centuries survive at Station Road, Erdington (an early seventeenth-century barn later converted into cottages), Old Rectory Farm, Sheldon (from 1690 to 1729 the

'Farm' now stands in inner city Sparkbrook but it was a country house when it was built in the 1740s for the Lloyd family, of banking fame.

Rookery House, Erdington (around 1725-30) is something of a mystery as it seems to contain elements of the plan of a mediaeval timber-framed hall with its off-centre door and slightly projecting wings. This is possibly because it took the place of one.

Old Rectory Farm, Sheldon was from 1690 to 1729 the home of Dr Thomas Bray, founder of the Society for the Promotion of Christian Knowledge.

Cole Hall Farm (now a pub) dates from around 1700 and shows an interesting mixture of features, some dating back to its timber-framed origins (a detached bake-house) and some up-to-the-minute (a classical L-shaped plan).

home of Dr Thomas Bray, the founder of the Society for the Promotion of Christian Knowledge), Wiggins Hill Farmhouse, Sutton Coldfield (early seventeenth century with Dutch gables), Cole Hall Farm (around 1700) and the remarkable Erdington Hovel of the late eighteenth century.

Faint glimpses of the village past in some of Birmingham's suburbs can still be seen. In Northfield there is the seventeenth-century village pound and timber-framed Great Stone Inn with its eighteenth-century brick facing. Harborne has the Bell Inn, an eighteenth-century pebbledashed timber-frame with original tile roof. While in Yardley, eighteenth- and nineteenth-century farm and village buildings survive near St Edburgha's church and the sixteenth-century timber-framed Old Trust School (see Chapter 2) in an area mercifully bypassed by modern roads and development.

Opposite: Moseley Hall Dovecote and the adjacent 'cowhouse' are all that remain of the eighteenth-century Moseley Hall destroyed in the Priestley Riots of 1791.

How the other half lived; the tiny late eighteenth-century Erdington Hovel is a remarkable survival of rural 'squatting' in a modern urban setting. This was identified by chance during redevelopment and saved by local campaigners.

The quaintest Georgian structure in Birmingham is the 'Gothick' (i.e. pretend Gothic) Perrot's Folly, built in what was then the open land of Rotton Park by John Perrot in 1758. Now hemmed in by nineteenth- and twentieth-century buildings, its parapet still offers excellent views over the city (on the occasions when it is open to the public) to those willing to climb the 139 steps to the top. There is, as mentioned in the previous chapter, another 'Gothick' tower at New Hall (1796).

The eighteenth century was also the period when purpose-built Nonconformist and post-Reformation Catholic places of worship began to appear in the city, but few have survived. Following destruction of the first Birmingham masshouse in 1689, Catholic worship was centred at the late

Opposite: Birmingham's quaintest eighteenth century building is without doubt Perrot's Folly, Edgbaston, now hemmed in by housing but in open country when built in 1758. Fans of Tolkien, who grew up in the area, believe it and the nearby waterworks tower (see Chapter 6) were the inspiration for the Two Towers from the *Lord of the Rings* trilogy.

seventeenth- or early eighteenth-century Masshouse in Pritchatts Road, Edgbaston. Catholicism returned to central Birmingham in 1786, with the building of the 'disguised' church of St Peter off Broad Street (demolished 1969). Oscott was the principal centre of Catholic worship with its post-Relief Act chapel (1788) and seminary (1794) at Maryvale, originally the home (rebuilt around 1753) of the persecuted seventeenth-century Catholic priest, Andrew Bromwich.

The earliest surviving Nonconformist place of worship in the city centre is the New Meeting of 1732, destroyed (or merely badly damaged?) in the

The Masshouse in Pritchatts Road, Edgbaston, where local Catholics found refuge while they were not welcome in Birmingham between 1689 and 1786.

Opposite: Although it is now, and has been since 1861, the Roman Catholic church of St Michael, this building started life as a Unitarian meeting house in 1732 and is thus the oldest surviving example in the city centre. It was either badly damaged or totally destroyed in the riots of 1791 against its minister, Joseph Priestley and reopened in 1802.

Soho House, Handsworth (now a museum) is, historically speaking, Birmingham's most important eighteenth-century building, as it was the home of that giant of the Industrial Revolution, Matthew Boulton, founder of the nearby Soho Manufactory.

Priestley Riots of 1791, reopened in 1802, and converted into the Roman Catholic church of St Michael in 1861. There is also a former Quaker meeting house of 1724, converted to a dwelling in the late eighteenth or early nineteenth century, on Wiggins Hill, Sutton Coldfield.

The city's most famous eighteenth-century building is Soho House in Handsworth, an unfinished mid-century dwelling enlarged and improved by founding father of the Industrial Revolution, Matthew Boulton, who lived there from 1766 to 1809. Designed by architects Samuel and James Wyatt, its many innovations included the first central heating system in Britain since Roman times, a flushing toilet and weather-resistant slate cladding painted to imitate ashlar. The house is now a museum of the Industrial Revolution.

INDUSTRIAL BUILDINGS

THIS CHAPTER DEALS with industrial buildings of the eighteenth century and earlier and specific industrial building types that evolved thereafter. Nineteenth- and twentieth-century industrial buildings that simply reflect the architectural style of their time are dealt with in the relevant chapters.

It is important to understand that Birmingham's industrial archaeology does not begin with the 'Industrial Revolution' period of the eighteenth century. Roman pottery kilns have been found in Perry Barr and Mere Green and there is also archaeological evidence of pottery manufacture in the Deritend area in the thirteenth century and a major leather industry in the Bull Ring area from the thirteenth to the eighteenth centuries. An important 'proto-industrial' site, the Aston Furnace (1615) awaits exploration in Newtown.

Aston Furnace was one of several sites along the Tame Valley that brought blast furnace technology, and with it the capacity for large-scale production of iron, to the area in the sixteenth and early seventeenth centuries. Many watermills were converted from agricultural use to industrial activity.

Sarehole Mill in Hall Green (1764-68 on the site of an earlier mill) and Newhall Mill, Sutton Coldfield (a brick building of around 1790 built on the stone foundations of an earlier mill of 1570-75) are the best preserved of the few surviving examples of over eighty watermills that once lined the small streams and rivers of Birmingham. There were once also over thirty windmill sites in the city but nothing remains save slight landscape features at the site of Wake Green Mill.

Sarehole Mill was briefly owned by founding father of the Industrial Revolution, Matthew Boulton. It may be that he saw it as a potential power-source for his planned new manufactory outside Birmingham. Whatever the case, he soon left, possibly because he had found a more reliable watermill at what was to become Soho in Handsworth.

Tragically, nothing remains of the epoch-making Soho Manufactory (1764), which was demolished and built over in the nineteenth century, and has since only been briefly visible, at foundation level, during the Channel Four *Time Team* dig of 1996. However, the Soho Foundry of 1796, where James Watt's steam engines were manufactured, survives relatively intact just outside the city in Smethwick and plans are afoot to make it into a major heritage site.

Soho and other similar works brought large-scale manufacturing industry to an area that had previously specialised in the 'agricultural' industries of tanning, smithing, nailmaking and the production of metal farm implements. These continued in the surrounding rural districts that now form the city's

Watermills were an important power source for early industries, and this one, Sarehole Mill, Hall Green was built in 1764-68 on the site of an earlier mill, briefly owned by Matthew Boulton and possibly considered as the site for his manufactory.

New Hall Mill, Sutton Coldfield is a classic two-and-a-half storey mill building from around 1790 on the site of an earlier mill from between 1570-75.

suburbs, where you will find, for example, an early nineteenth-century smithy in Yardley Village and eighteenth-century nailer's cottages and workshop in Northfield.

The steam technology developed at Soho soon superseded the waterpower that had made it all possible. One of James Watt's original 'single-action pumping engines' remains as the oldest working example in the world in the Discovery Centre at Millennium Point.

Birmingham can also claim a 'world's oldest' in another technology – gas. Although the use of gas as a power source was developed elsewhere (despite William Murdock's work in this field and his pioneering use of gas-lamps at Soho to celebrate the Peace of Amiens in 1802), the city has what may well be the oldest surviving gas-works building in the world in Gas Street (1822).

Following the municipalisation of gas in the 1870s, the same thing happened in the 1890s to the latest power technology – electricity. The 1906 Corporation Electricity Generating Station in Summer Lane is the best example of the structures devised for this purpose.

As large-scale industry grew in Birmingham at the likes of the long vanished Soho Manufactory, traditional agricultural industries retreated into the surrounding countryside, now the suburbs. These eighteenth-century nailer's cottages and workshop are in Northfield Village.

This anonymous building in Gas Street, the Retort House of 1822, may well be the world's oldest surviving gas works.

Birmingham's electricity generating stations are also now a source of historical interest – this example is in Summer Lane and dates from 1906.

The principal industries of eighteenth-century Birmingham – brass, jewellery and guns – have left little structural legacy, since most brass-works have been demolished (only the office frontage survives of the 1781 Brasshouse on Broad Street, now a pub) and the jewellery and gun trades were largely carried out in converted domestic properties on the Colmore (St Paul's) and Weaman (St Mary's) estates respectively. Furthermore, the Gun Quarter was subject to large-scale redevelopment in the 1960s, leaving only a few late eighteenth-/early nineteenth-century buildings on Loveday Street and Price Street and, from the same period, the former Lloyd & Son works on Princip Street, with house frontage and workshops behind. The block on Bath Street consists of an 1820s corner pub (now the Gunmakers Arms) at one end and an 1830s Wesleyan chapel at the other with 1840s workshops in between. In the 1870s these workshops were joined through to others on the adjacent Shadwell Street to form the Abingdon Works. The pride of the Gun Quarter is in fact on the other side of town: the 1813 Gun-Barrel Proof House (Jacobean-style gateway 1883) in Banbury Street.

Sadly, the 1781 Brasshouse in Broad Street (now a pub) is the only remnant of the industry that revolutionised eighteenth-century Birmingham.

The Jewellery Quarter has fared better with a number of surviving buildings (e.g. 69-70 Great Hampton Street) demonstrating the key evolutionary development whereby houses were converted into business premises and back-gardens infilled with workshops. The Pickering & Mayell building on Caroline Street is a classic example of an 1820s combination of house frontage and workshops behind.

The Jewellery Quarter also contains many buildings from the next stage of the city's industrial development, in the nineteenth century when, first, purpose-built workshops and, later, factories came into use. Nos. 22-46 Vittoria Street show a progression from converted 1840s back-to-backs through 1860s workshops to the 1890s Unity Works.

Just as the Gun Quarter had its Proof House so the Jewellery Quarter had its Assay Office. Founded in 1773, the present building in Newhall Street dates from 1878.

Given the dearth of surviving structures from the brass industry, it was a little surprising when a survey in the 1990s revealed traces of buildings relating to an industry not usually associated with the city – glassmaking.

Practically all that remains of the once proud Gun Quarter, scythed through by the Inner Ring Road in the 1960s, is this block on Bath Street and a few buildings in neighbouring Loveday Street and Price Street.

But the Gun Barrel Proof House (1813) is alive and well on the other side of town, in Banbury Street.

The classic Jewellery Quarter/Gun Quarter development pattern of a house taken over by the trade and its back garden infilled with workshops is best illustrated today by this example in Great Hampton Street (the back of the house is at the far end).

As the Gun Quarter had its Proof House, so the Jewellery Quarter had its Assay Office. The first opened in 1773 but this building in Newhall Street dates from 1878.

The office frontage of the 1815 Islington glassworks (now the Old Orleans pub), with the foundations of the glass cone believed to be buried in the car park behind, can be seen in Broad Street, while fragmentary remains of the Aston Flint Glassworks (in Bagot Street, near Dartmouth Circus) and the Belmont Glassworks (off Lawley Middleway, near Ashted Circus) are also extant.

Birmingham's greatest structural legacy from the 'Industrial Revolution' is undoubtedly its many miles of canals and railways. Gas Street Basin is at the heart of the national waterway network and Curzon Street station building is one of the most important pieces of railway architecture in the world.

Before the coming of the canals Birmingham had been dependent on an unreliable road network. This was only marginally improved by eighteenth-century 'turnpiking', which has left slight vestiges in the nineteenth-century turnpike milestones on the Hagley and Holyhead Roads and a single turnpike tollhouse of around 1800 at Colletts Brook Farm on the Tamworth Road outside Sutton Coldfield. The crossing of the River Tame at Perry Barr was improved by replacing the mediaeval wooden bridge with a stone 'zigzag'

Colletts Brook Farm on the Tamworth Road outside Sutton Coldfield is the city's last remaining turnpike tollhouse, dating from around 1800.

bridge in 1711 – it can still be seen beside its 1930s concrete replacement on the Aldridge Road. Another remnant of the era is the former coaching inn, the Three Tuns, in Sutton Coldfield.

The city has countless important canal structures, worthy of a book in themselves. Among the earliest are the Worcester & Birmingham Canal Co. offices and rare guillotine lock at Kings Norton Junction (1796). Original brick hump-backed bridges of the late eighteenth century survive at, among other places, Woodcock Lane, Acocks Green and Pritchatts Road, Edgbaston but more common are early nineteenth-century cast-iron bridges such as those around Farmer's Bridge Junction in the city centre. The cast-iron viaduct carrying the Worcester & Birmingham Canal across Holliday Street is particularly decorative.

The earliest canal-side buildings are possibly the cottages at Kingston Row beside the 1772 Newhall branch of the Birmingham Canal. The rival Birmingham Canal Navigations and Worcester & Birmingham Canal toll-houses side by side at Gas Street Basin date from around 1815 and 1893 (rebuild) respectively, while the Worcester & Birmingham Canal offices in Gas Street are 1876.

The Worcester & Birmingham Canal Company offices at Kings Norton Junction (1796) is one of Birmingham's earliest and finest canal structures. The tower and spire of Kings Norton Parish church (see Chapter 2) can be seen in the background.

The eighteenth-century canal junction at Farmer's Bridge remains at the heart of the city between the National Indoor Arena and the International Convention Centre.

One of the city's most remarkable canal-side structures is 'The Roundhouse' on the corner of Sheepcote Street and St Vincent Street. Sometimes wrongly referred to as a railway wharf of the 1840s, it is in fact an 1870s Corporation Stable and Stores.

Birmingham's canal age reached its peak with the creation of Rotton Park/Edgbaston Reservoir as the feeder for the entire system by the country's greatest engineer, Thomas Telford, in 1825-26. The Reservoir Lodge dates from around 1828, the dam brickwork and pumping station cottage (the pumping station itself having been demolished in the 1920s) from the 1830s and the buildings on the adjacent Icknield Port Loop from the 1840s (office and dock), '60s (stable block) and '90s (stores).

No sooner had the canal system been perfected with the opening of the Tame Valley Canal in 1844 than along came the railways!

In fact the railways arrived a few years earlier, leaving behind one of Birmingham's most important buildings, Curzon Street station. Designed by Sir Philip Hardwick and opened in 1838 as the terminus of the London and

The remarkable 'Roundhouse' at the corner of Sheepcote Street and St Vincent Street (now an entertainment venue) was once mistakenly believed to be an 1840s railway wharf but was in fact an 1870s Corporation Stables and Stores.

Rotton Park (now known as Edgbaston) Reservoir was designed by world-famous engineer Thomas Telford in the 1820s and still fulfils its function as the principal feeder to Birmingham's canals.

Curzon Street Station (1838), designed by Sir Philip Hardwick as the counterpoint to his Euston Arch, so notoriously demolished in the 1960s, is one of the most important railway buildings in the world.

Birmingham railway, it was the counterpart of the now notorious Euston Arch in London, whose demolition in the 1960s kick-started the modern conservation movement.

The viaducts leading to Curzon Street are historic monuments in themselves: in particular the Grand Junction Railway viaduct crossing Lawley Street with its original brickwork beneath and a second level of later blue brick above.

The fierce rivalry between railway companies is symbolised by the 'Duddeston' Viaduct (actually running through the streets of Digbeth) that was meant to link the London and Liverpool/Manchester lines but was never

The Grand Junction Railway Viaduct crossing Lawley Street was built originally in 1839 to serve a second Curzon Street station (the other being on the London and Birmingham line) and was heightened in the 1850s when New Street became the town's principal station.

completed due to a dispute over access. This monument to pigheadedness can be traced from Bordesley station, where it branches off the mainline, to its dead end in Montague Street.

Birmingham's central station moved from Curzon Street to New Street in the 1850s, but the latter was totally rebuilt in the 1960s. A similar fate befell the city's other mainline station, the Great Western Railway's Snow Hill, when it was demolished in the 1970s, only later to be rebuilt on the same site. An early twentieth-century glazed-brick wall and doorway with the GWR crest above survives in Livery Street.

Also from this period is the abandoned but still standing Moor Street station of 1909, built to serve the 'commuter' Birmingham, North Warwickshire & Stratford Railway (1907). Hall Green station (whose signal

Opposite: One of the few parts of old Snow Hill station, the GWR rival to New Street, to have survived demolition and total rebuilding is this doorway on Livery Street.

box now stands on the revived Gloucester Warwickshire Railway at Winchcombe) and Yardley Wood Halt are other well-preserved reminders of this line. Earlier suburban stations of particular historical or architectural interest are to be found at Acocks Green (1852) and Sutton Coldfield (1884).

By the later nineteenth century, trams were providing an alternative form of 'commuter' transport. The Aston Manor Tram Depot of 1882 on Witton Lane is now fittingly the home of the Aston Manor Road Transport Museum.

EARLY NINETEENTH-CENTURY BUILDINGS

Two HISTORICAL EVENTS, one local and the other national, make the transition between late eighteenth- and early nineteenth-century Birmingham buildings particularly marked. The first is the Priestley Riots of 1791, which saw the destruction of a number of large houses. When the Georgian brick Moseley Hall was rebuilt in 1799 it was in the fashionable Greek Revival stone style.

On a national level, the wars against France put the brakes for almost twenty years on the growth of new housing estates. When building resumed in the 1810s and '20s, exposed brick was no longer in vogue; in the words of the developers of the prestigious Bennetts Hill and Waterloo Street (1825-27) in the town centre: 'all houses or other erections shall be of stone, or coated with its semblance, Roman cement'.

Even in lower status housing, where exposed brick remained the norm, some changes in fashion were adopted. An interesting transition in door and window styles can be seen to the north of St Paul's Square, where building stopped in the 1790s. Two buildings in Caroline Street, one of the 1820s and the other of the 1830s, show how first segment-arched windows gave way to corniced 'mantelpiece' windows and then Georgian baroque doorcases were replaced by Classical Revival porches. The Brewmaster's House of around 1800 (now in the ICC complex) shows the first stage of this transition with 'mantelpiece' windows but an old style baroque doorcase. Some later houses have the cornices beneath the windows, as on the Alcester Road opposite Moseley Hall Hospital.

When Moseley Hall was rebuilt in 1799 following destruction in the Priestley Riots of 1791, brick was replaced by fashionable Greek Revival stone.

A window on history: late eighteenth-century styles in St Paul's Square give way, after twenty years interruption due to the Napoleonic Wars to...

...early nineteenth-century styles in Caroline Street – the building in the foreground is the Pickering & Mayell premises referred to in Chapter 4.

Ashfurlong Hall in Sutton Coldfield acts by way of architectural bookends to the age of brick. Here an early sixteenth-century stone Vesey House (see Chapter 2), extended around 1600, was redesigned into a Greek Revival mansion with central stone porch. The effect was later heightened when the Roman Ionic portico of demolished Moor Hall was brought in as a garden feature.

The epitome of Revival/Regency architecture in Birmingham is provided by the high-status Calthorpe Estate in Edgbaston, the home of the town's élite and since dubbed 'Brum's Belgravia'. Even here, early houses such as 60 Calthorpe Road (around 1800) at the Five Ways entrance to the estate are in brick; but you don't have to walk far along the road to find the white stucco frontages and Regency cast-iron railings that dominated the area from the 1810s.

The nearer you get to the heart of the estate, the bigger and grander are the houses, and there is also a wide range of Regency styles to be seen, from the ornate Roman Corinthian of 36 Calthorpe Road (1829-30) to the simple Classical, unadorned except for chinoiserie porches, of 4-5 Carpenter Road (around 1829). The largest Regency houses are on Wellington Road but these include some over-egged Victorian copies of the 1840s and '50s.

Much rarer than 'mantelpiece' windows are those with the cornices beneath, as in these examples on the Alcester Road in Moseley.

Birmingham's Belgravia: the Regency Calthorpe Estate has houses ranging from this simple dignified terrace with chinoiserie porches to…

...the grand mansions of Wellington Road.

The Calthorpes learned the lesson of the Colmore and other town centre estates by placing restrictions on the number of buildings per plot and excluding industry. They also established 'buffer' zones of lower middle-class housing to the north and east. The northern limit of the estate was protected still further from its town centre neighbours by the separate development of Lee Crescent, with far more modest Regency styles, in the 1830s. Then came the Edgbaston/Birmingham border and a stark contrast, perpetuated by the modern high-rise Lee Bank Estate that replaced it, with acres of back-to-back housing.

Tens of thousands of back-to-backs were being constructed in Birmingham at this time but almost none survive. One rather unusual block of the 1820s-30s, on the corner of Hurst Street and Inge Street (next to the Hippodrome), is being preserved as a heritage attraction, a valuable reminder that 'historic' buildings are not just those of the rich and famous.

Stuccoed Regency buildings are to be found on most of the main routes into the city, such as the 'Regency House' terrace (around 1825), now just a façade, on Hagley Road.

The Jewellery Quarter displays the impact of the age in all its aspects: 27 Frederick Street is a fine pair of Greek Revival houses of around 1830 with a typically over-the-top Victorian copy next door; Albion Street has rows of plain, white-fronted houses, later provided with large bay windows to increase light to the workshops within; the Regent Works and Victoria Works (both around 1837) are early examples of factory buildings in a symmetrical, round-cornered Classical style; this continues through to the 1860s with the Birmingham Mint on Icknield Street (1860-62).

The aforementioned Bennetts Hill and Waterloo Street have the ironic distinction of being the last part of the town centre to be built up (local historian Robert Dent pined in 1878 that he remembered children gathering blackberries 'where now nothing grows save interest and lawyers' bills') but the oldest still surviving!

Waterloo Street provides a fitting approach to Birmingham's oldest surviving public building (the 1807 Public Offices having long been demolished): the Roman Corinthian Town Hall, said to be based upon the Temple of Castor and Pollux in the Forum at Rome. Work started in 1832 but struggled on until the 1860s, a foretaste perhaps of the troubles afflicting the building at the turn of the Millennium.

The Victoria Works from around 1837 is an early example of a Birmingham factory (pen-making being one of the few local trades that required production line manufacture), very much in keeping with the architectural style of the times.

Regency Waterloo Street (1825-27) which, with Bennetts Hill (crossing it at this point) was the last part of the city centre to be built up, is now, ironically, the oldest surviving. It leads to...

Local architect Charles Edge, who took over the project following the bankruptcy of the original designer, Joseph Hansom, also built the Market Hall in the Bull Ring (1833-35), a second major public work by the Birmingham Street Commissioners, but this was demolished in the 1960s.

The Town Hall, Market Hall and Curzon Street Station (see Chapter 4) were an impressive trio of classical public buildings for the newly created Borough of Birmingham of 1838.

Amid all this classicism, Gothic architecture remained a rare oddity, with only a few quirky buildings adopting the style: the late-eighteenth-century castellated Wheatmoor Farmhouse, probably designed to be seen as a landscape feature from Ashfurlong Hall (see above); early nineteenth century Metchley Abbey, a pretence of mediaevalism built around an earlier farmhouse; Browne's Green Lodge in Handsworth (around 1810), a cottage orné and the Plough & Harrow, Hagley Road (1830s), in Tudor Gothic.

But that was all about to change with the coming to Birmingham of two major Gothic architects, Thomas Rickman and the grandfather of them all, Augustus Welby Northmore Pugin.

... Birmingham Town Hall, begun by Joseph Hansom (of Hansom Cab fame) in 1832 and completed by local architect Charles Edge, is said to be based on the Temple of Castor & Pollux in Rome, but since only three columns of the latter remain upstanding, this is hardly convincing.

Rickman has already been mentioned in Chapter 2 as the man who defined the different styles of mediaeval church architecture; but he was also an important architect in his own right, although opinions differ as to the quality of his buildings. He built in both styles, as evidenced by the surviving tower of the bombed Greek Revival church of St Thomas, Bath Row (1826-29) and his best local building, the Birmingham Banking Company (now HSBC) on the corner of Bennetts Hill and Waterloo Street (1830). But his true love was Gothic and he built four churches in this style: unfortunately for him and us, they were Commissioner's churches on a very low budget and, still worse, only one has survived, St Barnabas in Erdington (1822-24). His revolutionary use of cast-iron at St George's, Newtown (1820-23) copied from his earlier

Metchley Abbey is a rare example in Birmingham of early nineteenth-century 'Gothick' (i.e. pretend Gothic) – the pretensions of the name (there are no monastic connections) and style are fairly obvious.

The cast-iron gates and his tomb (visible between the trees) are all that remain of St George's, Newtown by one of Birmingham's nationally important architects, Thomas Rickman, the man who brought 'real' Gothic to the city in the 1820s.

church of the same name in Liverpool, can only be seen today in the form of the churchyard gates, the church itself having been demolished in 1960. Other lost Rickman churches are All Saints, Hockley (1832-33), Bishop Ryder Memorial, Gem Street (1837) and the Greek Revival St Peter, Dale End (1825-27). He also supervised the building of Bridgens' Watt Chapel at Handsworth (1826).

Rickman was neither the only church architect in early nineteenth-century Birmingham nor the only one to work for the Commissioners. Other such churches are: Holy Trinity, Bordesley (1820-22) by Francis Goodwin, loosely based on Kings College Chapel, Cambridge; St John, Perry Barr (1831-33) in Early English (chancel and transepts added around 1887); St George, Edgbaston (1836-38), also Early English (chancel added by Edge 1856, the nave and chancel rebuilt on a grander scale by Chatwin 1884-85); and (for the Birmingham Church Building Society) St Matthew, Duddeston (1839-40), a curious mixture in brick of Georgian and Early English.

Then there was Pugin! Birmingham is blessed with no fewer than five buildings or parts of buildings by the eccentric genius. His celebrated partnership with Charles Barry on the Houses of Parliament was in fact foreshadowed three years earlier by their work on King Edward's School, New Street (1833-37) – the Upper Corridor has been moved stone by stone to the school's new site in Edgbaston (see Chapter 7), where it now forms the War Memorial Chapel. At Oscott College (1835-38) he added the distinctive chapel interior and gatehouses to the otherwise uninspired Tudor edifice by Potter. His finest local work is undoubtedly St Chad's RC Cathedral (1839-41), in a fourteenth-century North German style. He later built the Convent of Our Lady of Mercy, Hunter's Road (1840-45 in Tudor Gothic) and the original mortuary chapel of St Joseph's RC, Nechells (1850, extended into a church by his son in 1870-72).

Unsurprisingly, many in the Catholic Church warmly welcomed the return of pre-Reformation Gothic, particularly in the hands of the convert, Pugin. An antiquarian priest helped in the planning of Charles Hansom's St Thomas and St Edmund of Canterbury/Erdington Abbey (1848-50). But there were those in the church who favoured Roman Classicism and they were led by Edgbaston-

Opposite: Rickman could also 'do' Classical as shown by the surviving Greek Revival tower of his St Thomas, Bath Row (1826-29), the rest of which was destroyed by bombing during the Second World War. It is now the centrepiece of the St Thomas Peace Gardens.

St Chad's RC Cathedral (1839-41) is the best of five Birmingham buildings by eccentric Gothic genius, Augustus Welby Northmore Pugin.

Pugin's taste for Gothic was not shared by everyone, even in his adopted Catholic church. Cardinal Newman's Oratory buildings on the Hagley Road (1850s-60s) and the early-twentieth-century Roman Renaissance church behind (1903-09 – see Chapter 7) reflect his preference for worshipping God in Classical surroundings.

based John Henry (later Cardinal) Newman, whose staunch opposition to Pugin put Birmingham in the front line of the 'Battle of the Styles'. His Oratory buildings (1850s-60s) on the Hagley Road are unashamedly Italian Renaissance and the church behind, built in his memory in the early twentieth century (see Chapter 7) is a little bit of Rome in Birmingham.

As seen above, the Anglican Church in Birmingham had also gone Gothic, but it found no architect to replace Rickman or match Pugin, with the possible exception of the 'rogue' Samuel Sanders Teulon, who built the quaint St James, Edgbaston (1852 – no longer a church) and the more conventional St John, Ladywood (1852-54) as well as the cottage named after him in Birmingham Botanical Gardens. The Norman church of St John the Evangelist, Walmley (1845 by D.R. Hill – see below) is described as 'a fascinating horror' by Pevsner.

Some Nonconformist sects held onto Classical a little while longer, as shown by the former Highbury Congregationalist (1844) in the Jewellery Quarter, now a Sikh temple, and Broad Street Presbyterian (1849), now 'The Church' night-club.

The Church of England too had gone Gothic. St James, Edgbaston (1852, no longer a church) is among the more interesting products; it is the work of 'rogue' Gothic architect, Samuel Sanders Teulon.

The entrance to Birmingham Workhouse (1850-52) on Western Road, Winson Green is (just about) still standing in the grounds of City Hospital as a reminder of the Dickensian days of local government in Birmingham.

The clash of styles continued even beyond death with a Classical mortuary chapel at Nonconformist Key Hill cemetery (1836) and a Gothic one in the Church of England's Warstone Lane (1848). Sadly neither survives but the cemeteries themselves are important landscape features with tombs cut into the sandstone ridge at Key Hill and still more impressive catacombs and a fine gatehouse at Warstone Lane.

Some types of buildings were more comfortable with Gothic than others, especially those that harped back to earlier religious or institutional traditions: schools (for example, Harborne C of E 1840, All Saints, Hockley 1843); colleges (Saltley C of E 1850-52, Spring Hill Congregational 1854-56, Handsworth Methodist 1880-81); almshouses (for example, Lench's Trust, Ladywood Middleway 1859). The ultimate institutional Gothic is to be found in Winson Green with its sorry trio of Gaol (1845-49, the 'toy fortress' by D.R. Hill, its castle gateway demolished in the 1980s), Asylum (also by Hill,

Opposite: Some Nonconformist churches held onto Classical as in the Presbyterian church (1849, now 'The Church' nightclub) on Broad Street.

The shock of the new. The career of Birmingham's most important Victorian architect, John Henry Chamberlain, got off to a bad start when he horrified local society by building a Venetian Gothic house amid the 'sham stucco' of the Regency Calthorpe Estate.

dated 1849 but with many extensions between 1851-78) and Workhouse (1850-52 by J.J. Bateman – only the gatehouse survives). The one institutional building to remain Classical was Queens Hospital on Bath Row (1840-41).

However, domestic architecture was much slower to follow the trend to Gothic and its arrival was to cause as great an uproar as any piece of modern architecture ever has.

In 1855 an unknown young architect from Leicester called John Henry Chamberlain built a Venetian Gothic house in Ampton Road, in the very heart of the Regency Calthorpe Estate. The reaction among local residents was one of horror and the young man struggled to find work in Birmingham for many years. But in the 1860s and '70s he was to emerge triumphant, applying his Ruskinian values to putting into bricks and mortar the political dreams of his namesake (but no relation), Joseph Chamberlain.

LATE NINETEENTH-CENTURY BUILDINGS

J ohn Henry Chamberlain was one of three local architects who, from the 1850s, led the transformation of Birmingham from a largely drab and dreary Georgian town (with a few notable exceptions) to a vibrant Victorian city. The others were Yeoville Thomason and Julius Alfred Chatwin.

While Chamberlain was going though his wilderness years, Thomason and Chatwin were beginning to make their mark.

Thomason followed up Chamberlain's Venetian Gothic Shenstone House with the North Italian redbrick Blucher Street Synagogue (1856), which in turn could be said to lead on, via G. Bidlake's Sutton Coldfield Town Hall (1859), to the magnificent Butterfield-style, polychrome brick Argent Centre (originally the Albert Works, 1860s by Bland).

Thomason then became involved in the rebuilding of Georgian Colmore Row in an Italian palazzo style – but the extent of this involvement beyond his best building, the Union Club (1869), is now being questioned. Here too, Chatwin appeared on the scene. Although he was to become famous (some would say infamous) for his many Gothic churches, his first important Birmingham building was the palazzo-style Joint Stock Bank (now a pub) on Temple Row (1862-4). He also did some good Classical work on refacing St Philip's (1864-69) and later extending its chancel (1883-84).

Birmingham's importance in banking (both Lloyd's and the Midland were founded here) is reflected in the Neo-Classical Midland Bank HQ, New Street (1865-69 by Edward Holmes, now a bookshop) and National Provincial (Westminster) Bank, Bennetts Hill (1869 by John Gibson, now a wine bar).

Where Chamberlain led, Yeoville Thomason followed, with his redbrick North Italian Blucher Street Synagogue (1856).

The 1860s saw the beginning of the end for a Scrooge-like generation of Birmingham councillors, whose only contribution to public building in almost thirty years of local government had been the aforementioned Gaol and Asylum in Winson Green. Forced belatedly to adopt the 1850 Free Libraries Act, the Council built the first Central Library and five branches between 1861-68, the sole survivor of which (although no longer a library) is Deritend Free Library on Heath Mill Lane (1866).

In the 1870s Chatwin and Thomason both played a part in the extension and aggrandisement of Colmore Row into one of Birmingham's major thorough-fares. At the east end, Chatwin built the French Renaissance Grand Hotel around 1875-78, possibly to a design by Plevins, later remodelled by Martin & Chamberlain between 1889-90. He also built the Italianate Great Western Hotel (1878, demolished 1976 – but W.H. Ward's Great Western Arcade of 1875-76, leading to it and constructed over the railway cutting to Snow Hill

Opposite: John Henry Chamberlain's Venetian Gothic Shenstone House, Ampton Road may have mortified the residents of the Regency Calthorpe Estate but it set the scene for the rebuilding of Birmingham in the 1870s to match the political ideals of his namesake, Joseph Chamberlain (Mayor 1873-76).

The Argent Centre, on the corner of Legge Lane and Frederick Street in the Jewellery Quarter (started 1862/63 as the Albert Works pen manufactory), is Butterfield-inspired polychrome brick. It stands on the site of the house where American author Washington Irving wrote *Rip Van Winkle* in 1818. The cost of building was partly met by opening fashionable Turkish Baths on the first floor, effectively getting people to pay to bathe in the steam generated by the pen-making machines!

station, still remains). At the west end Thomason built his masterpiece of brash eclecticism, the Council House (1874–79)

The building speaks volumes for the town's new-found confidence (if not its artistic taste!) under Joseph Chamberlain, who laid the foundation stone during his time as Mayor (1873–76). It contrasts sharply with the conventional redbrick vernacular of the Council House in Handsworth (then a separate authority) built at the same time (1878–79). Thomason added the Museum and Art Gallery, paid for from the profits of Chamberlain's municipalised Gas Department at the rear in 1881–85. The landmark clocktower at the end was intended as a rival to London's Big Ben. In 1880 the open space in front of the

Opposite: Gothic architect Julius Alfred Chatwin's first important Birmingham building was, somewhat surprisingly, the palazzo-style Joint Stock Bank on Temple Row (1862-64, now a pub). He also worked in the Classical idiom on nearby St Philip's church (now the Cathedral).

95

The 1860s rebuilding of Colmore Row in an Italian palazzo style marks the beginning of the transformation of Birmingham from a fairly drab Georgian town to a vibrant Victorian city. The Union Club in the foreground is generally considered to be Yeoville Thomason's best work.

Yeoville Thomason's Council House (1874-79) and Museum & Art Gallery (1881-85) symbolise Birmingham's brash new confidence in the era of Joseph Chamberlain.

Museum & Art Gallery was named Chamberlain Place (now Square) in honour of Joseph Chamberlain. The Chamberlain Memorial (a sort of miniature Albert Memorial) at its heart was designed by his namesake, John Henry.

John Henry Chamberlain had re-emerged after going into partnership in 1864 with William Martin, who had inherited, from D.R. Hill (see Chapter 5), the mantle of 'municipal' builder. They started with a series of highly acclaimed waterworks buildings: Edgbaston (late 1860s in polychrome brick), Longbridge (around 1870 – demolished) and Selly Oak (around 1875). But their greatest achievement in terms of social architecture was to build dozens of new Board Schools following the 1870 Education Act. Starting with Bloomsbury in 1873 (demolished), they had completed an incredible twenty-eight schools by 1880. Nor were these the shoddy quick-fixes found in other towns, including London itself, but 'the best building in the neighbourhood' with their landmark towers acting as both an aspirational symbol for the people in the crowded streets around them and part of a highly effective ventilation system. The most 'visible' of the schools is Oozells Street (1877), now

Martin & Chamberlain's greatest achievement was to build dozens of 'best building in the neighbourhood' Board Schools following the Education Act of 1870. This is Icknield Street, Hockley (1883).

the Ikon Gallery, but they are to be found, in varying states of repair, throughout the inner city, with particularly fine examples at Icknield Street (beside the Hockley flyover) and Summerfield on the Dudley Road.

John Henry Chamberlain could also build on the grand scale and he did this for his patron, Joseph, by creating a magnificent family home for him at Highbury in Moseley (1879-80). In the words of Pevsner 'He spared no effort (or expense) to produce a house worthy of the great man, and the result is a tour-de-force, with hardly an undecorated surface to be seen, and an impressive example of the use of a maximum number of media – wood, glass, tile, plaster, iron, granite – and patterns of flowers and birds to produce interiors of great heaviness and richness'.

Chamberlain's greatest triumph was his last – the Birmingham Municipal School of Art (1881-85), the country's first municipally owned institute of

Highbury (1879-80), the family home of the Chamberlain family, built by their namesake (but no relation), John Henry Chamberlain, is a 'tour-de-force', according to Pevsner.

Opposite: John Henry Chamberlain's 'comeback', in partnership with William Martin, started in the late 1860s/early 1870s with a series of much admired waterworks buildings including this one in Edgbaston, the other half of the Two Towers said to have inspired Tolkien (see Chapter 3).

higher education. Tragically he died on the very day that the design was accepted following a particularly virulent argument about the relative merits of Classical and Gothic architecture. Despite being relatively unknown outside Birmingham, it is possible to claim that he was one of the most illustrious casualties of the 'Battle of the Styles'. As Pevsner says 'In him Ruskin's political as well as artistic ideas were expressed with more fidelity than in almost any other architect'. It was truly fitting that his Venetian Gothic masterpiece, with its mixture of asymmetry, decorative variation and imitation of nature using stone, terracotta, mosaics and polychromatic tiles, should become the home of one of the country's leading schools of Arts & Crafts.

The one thing Chamberlain didn't build, it seems, was churches. St Stephen's, Selly Park (1870-71) is more Martin than Chamberlain; St Cyprian's, Hay Mills (1873-74), long seen by experts, possibly due to its passing resemblance to a Board School, to be Chamberlain, has recently been shown to be the work of another local architect, Frank Osborn; and St John the Evangelist, Sparkhill (1888) is post-Chamberlain.

The same can't be said – although some wish it could – of Chatwin, who had his finger in almost every Birmingham church building of the period. Dismissed by Little as a 'run of the mill revivalist', the Catholic Apostolic church on Summer Hill (1873, now the Greek Orthodox Cathedral) is considered his best, St Mark's, Washwood Heath (1894-99) about average, and people either love or hate the kitsch St Augustine's, Edgbaston (1868, tower and spire 1876). He is also either loved or loathed as the rebuilder/destroyer of mediaeval St Martin's-in-the-Bull-Ring (1873-75), St Mary, Handsworth (1876-80) and St Peter and Paul, Aston (1879-90). Neither was Yeoville Thomason above a bit of 'desecration', although his rebuilding of St Peter's, Harborne (1867) and the new north aisle of Holy Trinity, Sutton Coldfield (1875-79) are generally better received.

The preponderance of local church architects kept out the 'nationals' with the exception of J.L. Pearson, whose magnificent St Alban's, Conybere Street (1879-81) is only spoiled by the substitution due to money problems of a 1930s tower for the soaring spire he intended.

Opposite: The School of Art, Margaret Street (1881-85) was the country's first municipally owned institute of higher education and is also John Henry Chamberlain's masterpiece – tragically he died on the day his design was accepted.

The Greek Orthodox Cathedral (formerly Catholic Apostolic Church) on Summer Hill (1873). Is this Chatwin's best work or is it just the Eastern redecoration that makes it stand out?

Joseph Chamberlain's final dream before leaving local for national politics was the creation of a 'Parisian boulevard' running through the town centre. Unsurprisingly, his Corporation Street (1878-early twentieth century) was initially entrusted to Martin & Chamberlain; but an important change was to take place at its northern end after John Henry's death. The most prestigious building on the Street – the Victoria Law Courts (1887-91) – was contracted, not to a local architect, but a London one, Aston Webb. His redbrick and terracotta Renaissance palace, such a contrast to the outdated palazzo-style County Court (1882) next door, not only attracted national acclaim (it marked the end of the 'Stone Age' and beginning of the 'Terracotta Age' according to *The Builder* magazine) but also ushered in a period when Birmingham architecture was more influential than any time before or since.

Opposite: St Martin's: a once-in-a-lifetime glimpse of Birmingham's parish church unencumbered by surrounding buildings during redevelopment of the Bull Ring in 2001. Opinions are divided as to whether Chatwin's rebuilding of the mediaeval church in 1873-75 was rebirth or murder!

National architects were rarely used in Victorian Birmingham. J.L. Pearson's St Alban's, Conybere Street (1879-81), said to have been a strong influence on W.H. Bidlake (see below), is the exception to the rule.

But that was all to change with Aston Webb's Victoria Law Courts (1887-91), which revolutionised Birmingham architecture by introducing redbrick and terracotta.

Redbrick and terracotta was rapidly adopted by local firms including the post-Chamberlain Martin & Chamberlain, whose libraries (for example Small Heath and Spring Hill in 1893) take the Board School tradition to new heights and whose Bell Edison Telephone Building (1896) is a Grade I Listed Building. Less good are the General Hospital (1894-97 by W. Henman) and Methodist Central Hall (1903-04 by E. & J.A. Harper).

Buff terracotta was also much used, most delightfully in the County Buildings on Corporation Street (1897-99), whose original division into a furniture shop and vegetarian restaurant is reflected figuratively in the terracotta frieze. Other fine examples are 134 Edmund Street (1897), the Ruskin Buildings, Corporation Street (1899) and, out of town, Balsall Heath Library (1895 – adjoining Public Baths added in coarser style 1907).

'Tile and Terracotta' were the chosen materials for Birmingham's new 'respectable' public houses (replacing the earlier 'gin palaces') of which the main architects were William Jenkins (e.g. The Marlborough, Anderton Road, around 1900) and James & Lister Lea (e.g. The Bartons Arms, Aston, 1899-1901, The Red Lion, Soho Road in buff and plum terracotta 1901-2).

Where Aston Webb led, local architects followed; the Bell Edison Telephone Building on Newhall Street (1896) is Martin & Chamberlain's redbrick and terracotta masterpiece.

105

From one extreme to the other, churches too adopted the redbrick and terracotta look, the best being Thomas Proud's St Aidan's, Small Heath (1893-98) and St Barnabas, Balsall Heath (1898-1904).

It was the church architecture of this period which was to produce Birmingham's most respected architect, William Henry Bidlake, fittingly a product of Chamberlain's School of Art, whose St Agatha's, Sparkbrook (1899-1901) and St Andrew's, Handsworth (1907) are both Grade I Listed. He also built St Oswald's, Small Heath (1892-93, the west front was added in 1899), the Emmanuel, Sparkbrook (1901), Bishop Latimer Memorial, Winson Green (1903) and the Emanuel, Sutton Coldfield (1909-16) as well as various examples of domestic Arts & Crafts architecture (see Chapter 7).

The 'respectable' tile and terracotta Bartons Arms in Aston has the richest tiled interior of any Birmingham pub and is the work of prolific pub builders, James & Lister Lea.

Opposite: Probably Birmingham's greatest architect, William Henry Bidlake was a member of John Henry Chamberlain's School of Art, a centre of national importance for the Arts & Crafts movement; St Agatha's, Sparkbrook (1899-1901) – aptly enough with a Martin & Chamberlain Board School beside it – is considered his best work.

107

Having started the 'Red Revolution' with his Victoria Law Courts, Aston Webb returned to Birmingham in 1900-1909 to build the university in another new style, Byzantine Romanesque.

The century ends and a new one begins with another important intervention by Aston Webb, who, having previously started the 'red revolution', now, with his D-shaped central block and campanile-style Chamberlain Tower of the new University of Birmingham (1900-09) brought Byzantine Romanesque influences to the city.

Opposite: Buff terracotta became more popular at the end of the century; this delightful example on Corporation Street (the County Buildings, 1897-99) was originally split between a furniture shop and a vegetarian restaurant, hence the mixture of carpenters and diners on the terracotta frieze.

TWENTIETH-CENTURY BUILDINGS

B EFORE ASTON WEBB started work on the University, another nationally important architect had left his mark on Birmingham, constructing a building that spanned the nineteenth and twentieth centuries. But unlike the landmark university, standing high on its hill, this one is hardly noticed by the people of the city, despite being Grade I listed. The former Eagle Insurance Building at 122-124 Colmore Row could easily be mistaken for just another office block until you realise that, with a date of 1900, it is among the first. It is also a rare example of an actual building by Arts & Crafts guru and theorist William Lethaby, with deep meaning in design and decoration, of which Hickman asserts: 'This landmark in the history of architecture returns to the primitive to herald the future'.

A more domestic form of Arts & Crafts was fittingly to be the dominant style in what is arguably Birmingham's greatest contribution to social architecture: Bournville. Based around the Cadbury factory established in 1879, the village, begun in 1894, set new standards in quality of housing and green spaces, and inspired the century's Garden City movement. The principal architect was Alexander Harvey, who designed the village centre and its principal buildings (Friends Meeting House 1905, Junior Schools 1902-05, Rest House 1914) as well as setting the pattern for the style and layout of the housing.

Opposite: The Eagle Insurance Building in Colmore Row (1900) may seem at first glance to be an unlikely candidate for a building of national importance but its design by Arts & Crafts guru William Lethaby, with its strange mixture of myth and mathematics, makes it a pivotal piece of architecture.

Bournville Village Green, designed by Alexander Harvey with, in the foreground, his 1914 Rest House. Said to have been modelled on the Market Hall in Dunster, Somerset where the Cadburys spent their holidays; the village inspired the garden city movement of the twentieth century.

Bournville's houses, such as these in Holly Grove, set new standards for quality of building and gardens.

This delightful little Fire Station in Acocks Green (next to the Police Station of 1909 and opposite the Redbrick and Terracotta Baptist Hall of 1903) survived the threat of demolition in the 1990s.

Arts & Crafts suburbia is also to be found in Acocks Green (Sparkhill Council House 1902, Baptist Hall 1903, County Primary School 1909, Police Station 1909, Fire Station 1911), Harborne (Moor Pool Estate developed by Harborne Tenants Ltd from around 1908) and especially Four Oaks, Sutton Coldfield, the early twentieth century equivalent of the Calthorpe Estate. It has the same mix of large villas at the core – including some designed by C.E. Bateman ('Redlands', Hartopp Road) and Bidlake ('Woodgate', 37 Hartopp Road, 'Withens', 5 Barker Road) – with more modest housing at the edges (e.g. Anchorage Road).

Large Arts & Crafts houses exist throughout the city. Notable examples include: Winterbourne (1903 by J.L. Ball with important botanic gardens at the rear) and The Garth (1900 by Bidlake) both on Edgbaston Park Road; Archibald House (the original Westhill College, 1911 by Harvey); and buildings on Woodbourne Road, Edgbaston.

The most important churches of the period, apart from the ones by Bidlake mentioned in the previous chapter, are the Arts & Crafts St Peter's, Maney (1904-05 by Cossins, Peacock and Bewlay) and the Roman Renaissance

Church of the Immaculate Conception at The Oratory (1903-09 by Doran Webb), a symbol of the late Cardinal Newman's devotion to Roman rather than Gothic architecture (see Chapter 5).

Terracotta had a last flourish in the first decade of the century, in Edwardian Baroque buildings such as the Digbeth Institute (1908) and nearby Digbeth Police Station (1912) but was already being replaced by its glazed form, faience (e.g. The Trocadero, Temple Street c.1902, the Piccadilly Arcade, New Street 1909, originally a picture house, the Gwenda Works, Legge Lane 1913), and glazed brick (e.g. Moor Street Station 1909).

In Birmingham as elsewhere the flamboyance of Edwardian architecture came to a sorry end amidst the horrors of the First World War. However, the war was to leave the city a remarkable architectural legacy: the Austin Village,

The First World War brought an end to flamboyant Edwardian styles but left one important architectural legacy in the shape of the Austin Village, made up of pre-fabricated Canadian cedar-wood chalets imported from America – they provide comfortable accommodation to this day.

Opposite: In the first decade of the twentieth century, terracotta was being replaced by its glazed version, faience. The Piccadilly Arcade in New Street (1909) was originally an early cinema, echoing the Georgian décor of the since demolished Theatre Royal next door.

near the car factory in Longbridge, consisting of pre-fabricated Canadian cedar wood chalets (interspersed with brick buildings as firebreaks) imported from America to accommodate the expanded wartime labour force.

A different and, it could be argued, more sombre architecture followed the war, and continued through the economic depression of the late 1920s and early '30s. The trend towards Byzantine Romanesque started by Webb at the University (see Chapter 6) was adopted by church architects (for example, St Germain, Edgbaston, 1915-17 by E.F. Reynolds, St Francis, Bournville, 1925 by Harvey)

The Hall of Memory, commemorating those who died in the war (1923-24 by S.N. Cooke & W.N. Twist – the accompanying loggia of 1925 by the same architects is now in the St Thomas Peace Gardens, Bath Row), heralded two decades of white Neo-Classical public buildings culminating in the unfinished Baskerville House (1938). Its monolithic style and Roman imperial imagery, so reminiscent of Hitler's Germany and Mussolini's Italy, were not so popular by the end of the next war!

The architect who designed Baskerville House, T. Cecil Howitt, had previously built the Head Office of one of the city's greatest social achievements of the inter-war years, the council-owned Birmingham Municipal Bank. His Neo-Classical building in Broad Street (1931-33) contrasts with the domestic Queen Anne style of the bank's local branches.

Neo-Classical is also very much the style of the city's new office blocks of the 1930s, for example the Legal & General (1931 by S.N. Cooke) and Neville House (1934 by W.N. Twist), both in Waterloo Street – although these also contain futuristic elements.

But the dominant architecture of the period is that of Suburbia. Enormous housing estates, some as big as towns, developed on the edges of the expanding city. Weoley Castle, with its sinuous contoured layout and plentiful greenery (inspired by Bournville) was among the earliest, and Kingstanding the biggest. At first deprived of local amenities, the estates were later provided with shops and other public facilities.

Arts & Crafts clung on longer in Birmingham suburbia than almost anywhere else in the country, particularly in the hands of H.W. Hobbiss, who built, for example, The Antelope, Stratford Road (around 1921).

Typical of the age are middle class semis (such as School Road, Hall Green), shopping centres (for example Castle Square, Weoley Castle from around

The Hall of Memory (1923-24 by S.N. Cooke and W.N. Twist), built to commemorate the victims of the First World War, heralded two decades of white (Portland stone) Neo-Classical public buildings, ending with...

Baskerville House (1938 by T. Cecil Howitt). Its Roman Imperial symbolism, including fasces (bundles of sticks carried by Roman magistrates, from which fascism took its name) went rapidly out of fashion during the Second World War.

117

Typical houses on the 1920s/30s Weoley Castle Estate. Inspired by Bournville, it was one of many large suburban developments built at the time.

1930), roadhouse pubs (for example, The Black Horse, Northfield, 1929), garages (for example, Smithfield Garage, Digbeth, 1923), bus depots (Acocks Green, 1928), fire stations (for example, Cotteridge, 1930), electricity sub-stations (for example, Belchers Lane, Bordesley Green, 1930), hospitals (such as the Queen Elizabeth 1933-38), and cinemas, most famously the Art Deco Odeons of Birmingham entrepreneur, Oscar Deutsch, designed by his architect, Harry Weedon (for example, Kingstanding, 1935).

Architecturally speaking, Birmingham's most important building of this period is probably the German-inspired Art Deco Barber Institute of Fine Arts (1935-39 by Robert Atkinson) on the University campus. However, it might be argued that far more influential and forward-looking was the streamlined Brearley Street Nursery School (1938) by William Benslyn, who went on to build the modernist Dorrington Road School (1940) and Cherry Orchard Road School (1947). Convention and conservatism hung on in more traditional schools such as the Bluecoat School, Harborne (1930 by Ball and Simister) and King Edward's, Edgbaston, (1940 by H.W. Hobbis) – both following moves out from the city centre – and also in churches such as the Byzantine St Edmund, Tyseley, (1939-1940) by H.W. Hobbiss, and the Gothic Sacred Heart and Holy Souls RC, Acocks Green, (1940) by G.B. Cox.

The Odeon, Kingstanding (1935 by Harry Weedon), in the instantly recognisable Art Deco style of the famous chain of cinemas founded by Birmingham entrepreneur, Oscar Deutsch. Supposedly, Odeon stands for 'Oscar Deutsch Entertains Our Nation'.

The Barber Institute of Fine Arts (1935-39 by Robert Atkinson) on the campus of Birmingham University was inspired by contemporary German architecture and is probably the city's most important 1930s building.

Brearley Street Nursery School (1938) is a little-known gem by modernist architect, William Benslyn, with the streamlined shape of an ocean liner.

The Second World War has left a limited legacy of anti-aircraft emplacements, pillboxes and tank traps, while its immediate aftermath is represented by a row of surviving (and still inhabited) pre-fabs in Wake Green Road, Moseley, which, due to their being the only remaining council-owned ones of around 4,500 built, are now listed buildings. When post-war rebuilding started in the late 1940s and early '50s, it was in a whole new style of modern architecture with glass, zigzags and curves, the fullest expression of which (although more at home in Regent Street or even Paris or Rome) is Grosvenor House on New Street (1953, by Cotton, Ballard & Blow). The boom years of the 1950s saw the coming of big new department stores (for example, Marshall & Snelgrove, New Street – now the Britannia Hotel, 1955, by Guy North, and Rackhams, Corporation Street, 1957 by T.P. Bennett & Son), high-rise flats (for example, Hawkesley Farm Moat Estate, 1958, by A.G. Sheppard Fidler – built within and around the mediaeval moat mentioned in Chapter 2) and out-of-town shopping malls (for example, Kent's Moat Shopping Centre, 1955, also by Sheppard Fidler).

Wake Green Road, Moseley: the last remaining of around 4,500 prefabs put up in Birmingham at the end of the Second World War are now listed buildings.

Grosvenor House (1953 by Cotton, Ballard & Blow) on the corner of New Street and Bennetts Hill is the most flamboyant of Birmingham's 1950s commercial buildings.

Industrial buildings too followed the trend, a good example being the now derelict C. Combridge Ltd, Wrentham Street (1948 by Rudolf Frankel).

Post-war Modernism 'erupted' in the 1960s. The most recognisable building of this period is the Rotunda (1964-65 by James Roberts), designed to finish the curve of his Smallbrook Queensway (around 1960). Although considered an eyesore by many when new, it has since become the city's totem, receiving huge public support when threatened with demolition as part of the redevelopment of the Bull Ring and voted Birmingham's top landmark in a newspaper poll in 1993.

The most influential architectural firm in 1960s and '70s Birmingham was John Madin Design Group who were responsible for the Chamber of Commerce, Harborne Road (1960), the Birmingham Post and Mail Building (1965), the Warwickshire Masonic Temple (1970), the Central Reference Library (1973 – unfortunately for a library it has always leaked!), Neville House, Hagley Road (1976), and the National Westminster Bank, Colmore Row (1976).

Other key 1960s buildings are: Midlands Arts Centre (1964 by Jackson & Edmonds); St Matthew, Perry Beeches (1964 by Maguire & Murray – according to Pevsner 'A really important modern church'); St Catherine of Siena RC, Bristol Street (1964-65 by Harrison & Cox); Minerals & Physical Metallurgy building, University of Birmingham (1966 by Arup Associates); Signal Box, New Street station (1966 by Bicknall & Hamilton); Telecom Tower (around 1966); Bank of England, Temple Row (1967 by Fitzroy Robinson & Partners); Pebble Mill BBC Television Centre (around 1968); and, by way of complete contrast, the traditional Serbian church of St Lazar, Bournville (1968).

Modernism, with an increasing dose of brutalism, continued to hold sway in the 1970s: Carrs Lane Church Centre (1970 by Denys Hinton & Partners); the New Rep (Birmingham Repertory Theatre, 1971 by Graham Winteringham); Alpha Tower (1972 by Richard Seifert & Partners); St Anne's, West Heath (1975 by H.M. Wright). It was also the era of the out-of-town National Exhibition Centre (1976).

But there was to be a backlash to all this modernism and the large-scale demolition of old buildings to make way for it. The conservation movement –

Opposite: The Rotunda (1964-65 by James Roberts) was considered an eyesore when first built but is now a much-loved city landmark.

and in particular the Victorian Society – arrived on the scene just in time to save Colmore Row from incorporation into the city's Inner Ring Road (with the loss of buildings such as Lethaby's Eagle Insurance). The city's first Conservation Area was designated in 1969 (sadly too late to save the eighteenth century St Peter's RC church at its heart) and fourteen more followed in the next ten years. 1970 saw the establishment of the council's Conservation Areas Advisory Committee. Demolition of the old Reference Library (1879 by Martin & Chamberlain) in advance of the new Central Library marked an end to unrestrained redevelopment (although the fight goes on!) with the General Post Office in Victoria Square (1891) and Spring Hill Library (see Chapter 6) among the first to be saved. A new threat has emerged in the form of 'facadism', the preservation of the frontages of historic buildings but with the rest knocked down and rebuilt. This has happened, for example, to the central portion of Colmore Row (see Chapter 6), King Edward VII Children's Hospital, Ladywood Middleway (1913-17) and the Regency terrace on Hagley Road mentioned in Chapter 5.

No one has yet produced an architectural study of Birmingham buildings of the 1980s and '90s. From the point of view of the development of the city, key buildings are those reflecting the multi-cultural nature of modern Birmingham (for example, the Central Mosque, Belgrave Middleway, the Ghamkol Sharif Central Mosque, Golden Hillock Road and the Sri Dashmesh Sikh Temple, Soho Road) and those illustrating the city's reinvention of itself as a centre for business and tourism, (for example the Hyatt Regency Hotel, the International Convention Centre, and the National Indoor Arena).

Much of the city's newest architecture mixes modern and traditional styles. This can be post-modern kitsch to the extreme as in the extension built on the back of the GPO building when it was converted to the offices of the TSB (later Lloyds) in 1991 but can also provide exciting new buildings in the correct vernacular setting as in Brindley Place.

And finally, a new millennium of Birmingham buildings has dawned with the opening of the unashamedly modernist Millennium Point (a museum and visitor centre) in 2001.

Opposite: Alpha Tower (1972 by Richard Seifert & Partners) is a streamlined, almost aerodynamic building in contrast with the stark, concrete 'brutalism' of the period.

The Sri Dashmesh Sikh Temple in Soho Road, Handsworth is typical of the multi-cultural architecture of modern Birmingham.

Brindley Place combines modern architecture with a vernacular suited to its canal-side setting and offers hope for the future!

FURTHER READING

Cooke, Sue, Fenoughty, Sue, and Pounce, Erica (editors), *The Child's Vanishing Landscape: A Storybook about Listed Buildings*, Brewin Books, 1993

Coxon, Nicola, *Birmingham Terracotta*, Birmingham City Council, 2001.

Coxon, Nicola and McGregor, Sheila, *Discovering Deco, A 1930s architectural trail around Birmingham City Centre*, Birmingham City Council, 1994.

Coxon, Nicola, McGregor, Sheila and Upton, Chris, *Architecture & Austerity: Birmingham 1940-1950*, Birmingham City Council, 1995.

Coxon, Nicola and McGregor, Sheila, *Finding the Fifties, A 1950s architectural trail around Birmingham City Centre*, Birmingham City Council, 1996.

Coxon, Nicola and McGregor, Sheila, *Signalling the Sixties, 1960s Architecture in Birmingham*, Birmingham City Council, 1997.

Coxon, Nicola, *Shaping the Seventies, 1970s Architecture in Birmingham*, Birmingham City Council, 1998.

Crawford, Alan, Dunn, Michael and Thorne, Robert, *Birmingham Pubs 1880-1939*, Alan Sutton, 1986.

Dent, Robert Kirkup, *The Making of Birmingham: Being a History of the Rise and Growth of the Midland Metropolis*, J.L. Allday, 1894.

Hickman, Douglas, *Birmingham*, Studio Vista, 1970.

Leather, Peter, *A Brief History of Birmingham*, Brewin Books, 2001.

Little, Bryan, *Birmingham Buildings: the Architectural Story of a Midland City*, David & Charles, 1971.

Pevsner, Nikolaus and Wedgwood, Alexandra, *Warwickshire* (The Buildings of England), Penguin, 1966.

Stephens, W.B. (editor), *A History of the County of Warwick, Volume VII: The City of Birmingham (Victoria History of the Counties of England)*, Oxford University Press, 1964.

The Birmingham Sites and Monuments Record

The principal source of information on the over 2,000 locally or nationally listed buildings in the City of Birmingham is the *Birmingham Sites and Monuments Record* (SMR), a publicly accessible database maintained by Birmingham City Council Department of Planning's Conservation Group. Application to access the SMR can be made by letter, phone, fax or email.

An extensive bibliography of historic buildings and archaeological sites in Birmingham is given in my chapter on 'The Historic Environment' in Chinn, Carl (editor): *Birmingham: Bibliography of a City*, University of Birmingham Press, 2002.

Building History is a course run by the University of Birmingham for people of all ages and backgrounds. Participants learn about the historic buildings of Birmingham and the methods used to study them. They then undertake simple research projects on buildings, which they choose for themselves in consultation with the City Council's Department of Planning Conservation Group. This ensures that the buildings studied have not been done before and students' efforts will therefore make a significant addition to Birmingham's heritage (as was the case with St Cyprian's church, Hay Mills and Colletts Brook Farm tollhouse, both featured in this book). Completed projects are deposited with Birmingham Central Library (Local Studies & History Department) and in the files of the Conservation Group. Lists of completed projects appear in local history journal, *The Birmingham Historian*.